THE
INTERNATIONAL
MONETARY SYSTEM

THE INTERNATIONAL MONETARY SYSTEM

History, Institutions, Analyses

Robert J. Carbaugh and Liang-Shing Fan

THE UNIVERSITY PRESS OF KANSAS
Lawrence, Manhattan, Wichita

Library of Congress Cataloging in Publication Data

Carbaugh, Robert J.   1946-
    The international monetary system.

    Bibliography: p.
    Includes index.
    1. International finance. 2. Currency ques-
tion. 3. International liquidity. I. Fan, Liang-
shing, 1932-   joint author. II. Title.
HG3881.C29   332.4'5   75-38829
ISBN 0-7006-0141-4

Preface

International monetary reform is of vital importance to the countries of the world. Although many studies have been made of the structure and problems of the international payment mechanism, few provide an analytical survey of the international monetary system.

This study analyzes the structural and operational limitations of past systems as well as the major reform proposals for modifying and/or replacing the current system with a new payment mechanism. The intended outcome of this study is a comprehensive synthesis and extension of existing theories and analyses.

The structure and nature of the international payment system is described and the issues relating to international adjustment, liquidity, and confidence are identified. This is followed by a discussion of the nature of international liquidity; included is a description of liquidity's purpose, sources of demand and supply, and potential shortcomings. Another important issue analyzed is the theoretical and empirical implications of the gold standard. Of primary concern is the extent to which the actual operations of the system corresponded to the theoretical role of the gold standard, and the nature and limitations of the so-called dollar-gold system that prevailed in the past quarter century until 1971.

The major reform proposals of the international payment mechanism are next discussed. Included are the proposals of historical interest such as Keynes, Triffin, Bernstein, Stamp, Angell, Rueff, and the currently debated issues of the Special Drawing Rights standard, freely floating exchange rates, and the wider-band and crawling-pegged exchange rate mechanisms. Finally the study analyzes the nature, operation, and future role of the managed float exchange rate system, which resulted from the international monetary crisis of 1973. Of particular interest are the effects of the Organization of Petroleum Exporting Countries' (OPEC) cartel on the U.S. dollar as a reserve currency, and the monetary effects of the cartel's balance-of-payments surplus on the world financial markets.

The international monetary system has been evolving continuously in various world environments so that there is an unwritten and unfinished chapter to this monograph. We hope that our effort has provided readers enough information to analyze the current and future conditions.

We would like to thank Professors T. Ozawa, R. B. Held, and R. R. Keller for valuable comments. Mr. Herbert V. Prochnow and Professor Peter Frevert also provided many useful comments for improving the presentation.

R. J. C.
L. S. F.

Contents

CHAPTER 1

Introduction

The future success of the international payments mechanism has been a vital topic of discussion and examination by both academicians and policymakers in recent years. Throughout the 1950s and 1960s the international monetary mechanism was based upon the dollar-gold system, in which the U.S. dollar with gold were primarily sources of international reserves. After the August 15, 1971, U.S. suspension of gold convertibility for foreign official holders of outstanding dollar liabilities, the world was temporarily on a dollar standard. At the 1973 Nairobi meetings of the International Monetary Fund countries, a general outline was established for reforming the international payment mechanism; it was also agreed that a more lasting reform agreement should be reached when the Fund countries meet regularly. However, no final and definitive system has been agreed upon as yet.

The need for international monetary reform became critical when it became evident that the dollar-gold system suffered from several inherent defects. First, the balance-of-payments adjustment mechanism was often unsuccessful in assisting countries to attain external balance. Second, there was no adequate method of ensuring a long-run growth of international reserves that would be consistent with global needs; fears of liquidity shortages became widespread during the 1960s and early 1970s. Third, because international reserves largely consisted of U.S. dollar liabilities in addition to gold, there was a potential danger of disruptions in confidence and shifts among the existing reserve assets. These interrelated problems became known as the adjustment problem, liquidity problem, and confidence problem.

The purpose of this study is to provide an analytical survey of the international monetary system, primarily from the perspectives of international adjustment, liquidity, and confidence. Whereas some writers have discussed the payment mechanism on strictly theoretical grounds, and others have provided empirical descriptions of current and past monetary issues, this study attempts to make a theoretical and empirical analysis of the current and past system's strengths and weaknesses. Besides investigating these issues, an evaluation will be made of contemporary and historical monetary reform proposals. The methodology used in this study consists of the conventional tools of economic analysis. In the theoretical chapters, graphical and numerical examples are employed, while the empirical sections utilize descriptions of monetary systems and reform proposals.

This study is composed of seven chapters, the first of which is this brief introduction. Chapter 2 is an overview of the problems associated with the international monetary system, and it identifies the vital issues of adjustment, confidence, and liquidity. Chapter 3 further discusses the nature and problems of international liquidity. Chapter 4 provides a historical analysis of the gold standard; of central interest is the extent to which the gold standard's actual operation corresponded to the theoretical gold standard. Chapter 5 is a theoretical and empirical investigation of the dollar-gold system. Chapter 6 evaluates the major contemporary and historical proposals for reforming the international monetary system. Chapter 7 provides a summary and conclusions of the recent international monetary reform agreements as well as an analysis of the current operation and future role of the managed floating exchange rate mechanism.

CHAPTER 2

Statement of Issues

INTRODUCTION

This chapter presents an overview of the International Monetary Fund (dollar-gold system) by introducing its nature and briefly explaining in a political-economic framework the issues relating to international adjustment, liquidity, and confidence.

Since international trade generally differs from domestic trade in geographic, political, and monetary dimensions, a basic objective of an international payments mechanism is to ensure the coordination and interaction of economies separated by these frontiers. In attaining this goal, the international monetary system attempts to perform several functions similar in appearance to those of national monetary systems, but substantially different in content.[1] The first function of an international monetary system is that of promoting the accumulation of reserves. No precise theory is involved because normative issues involving political judgments, different national views on what constitutes proper reserve balances, and confidence in the international payments mechanism exert substantial influence. There exists no real method of determining a normal level of reserves. Providing a high-quality standard of value is a second function. As will be explained in the following chapter, because different reserve assets fulfill this function in varying degrees, there is a source of potential instability. A third function is to provide a means of settlement among central banks which facilitates the financing of imbalances in payment positions. However, prolonged disequilibriums are unacceptable, especially to deficit nations. (First, a deficit tends to be deflationary, disrupting the stability of an economy. Second, deficits often result in costly corrective external and internal adjustment measures. Third, deficits may "tax" other countries of their real goods and services.) In an attempt to fulfill these functions other normative issues must be considered: nationalistic goals involving domestic policies, the autonomy of a nation's internal balance (internal balance refers to a fully employed, noninflationary economy, while external balance implies balance of payments equilibrium; overall balance implies the simultaneous achieving of internal and external balance), and the degree of freedom desired in international transactions.[2] The effects of international adjustment, confidence, and liquidity largely determine the extent to which these aims and functions can be achieved.

ADJUSTMENT MECHANISM

The need for balance-of-payments adjustments arises from disequilibrium payment positions. Suppose a nation faces prolonged balance-of-payments deficits. The capacity to finance a deficit is limited by the stock of international reserves and the willingness of other nations to accept these balances; continued deficits ultimately impose pressures to eliminate the disequilibrium. A nation experiencing surplus balance-of-payments positions year after year may face undesirable economic growth rates, stimulating the rate of inflation. Surplus nations should adjust to eliminate disequilibriums although, unlike deficit nations, the incentive for the restoration of equilibrium does not tend to be as pronounced. The essential point is that prolonged balance-of-payments surpluses or deficits are inefficient and must eventually be removed.[3]

The adjustment mechanism is concerned with the transition to equilibrium after the initial equilibrium has been disrupted. Criteria that might be used to judge the efficiency of an adjustment mechanism include the following: a nation's external disequilibrium should not promote excessive costs, including inflation, deflation, or the disruption of international trade; maximum sustainable expansion of trade and payments should be enhanced.[4]

The process of adjustment is characterized by two interdependent dimensions—speed and magnitude. The speed of adjustment relates to the amount of time required to reallocate resources to equilibrium positions; the type of adjustment policy utilized influences the time needed to restore equilibrium. Measuring the extent to which resource allocation must occur is a dimension of magnitude. Among the variables affecting the speed and magnitude of adjustment are the exchange rate, national income levels, employment, domestic and foreign price levels, income distribution, the interest rate, productivity, and institutional factors such as a nation's goals and economic-political policies. The process of adjustment is multilateral in that both surplus and deficit countries must share the impact; it requires monetary inflation or currency revaluation by surplus countries, the opposite occurring in deficit countries.[5] The process of adjustment takes two major forms: under certain conditions balance-of-payments equilibrium may be restored automatically; however, if automatic adjustment is incomplete, discretionary government policies may be needed. Under a system of fixed exchange rates, automatic adjustment operates primarily upon domestic price and income changes. Conflicts of opinion about adjustment analyses often arise due to the relative importance attached to these effects.

Geared toward long-run equilibrium, the classical system adopted a theory of adjustment based directly upon changes in relative prices and indirectly upon holdings of monetary reserves in the forms of gold and foreign exchange. As will be discussed in Chapter 4, under this price-specie-flow mechanism, a deficit nation would find its monetary reserves shrinking, thus lowering the quantity of money and inducing lower prices. This would tend to make the deficit country's exports more competitive to the world and cause the deficit country to substitute domestically produced goods for imports in its purchases, therefore reducing the disequilibrium. The result was a long-run equilibrium theory based upon the automatic preservation of equilibrium by the monetary and price system.[6]

In contrast to the price-specie-flow mechanism, the Keynesian income-species-flow mechanism is based upon rigid prices and variable incomes, and stresses the possibilities of uncertainty and underemployment equilibrium. The income theory holds that adjustment may be automatic while incomplete. Since successful adjustment in the case of a deficit nation implies falling levels of income and employment, the income approach recognizes that economic policies are not necessarily solely governed by international forces but are closely geared toward national economic objectives. Considering noninflationary full employment a national aim, deficit nations may refuse to deflate while surplus nations may refuse to allow inflation, thus preventing adjustment. Protecting national objectives at the cost of external imbalance may lead to a disequilibrium of the system in the long run.[7]

Since a major shortcoming of relying on an automatic adjustment mechanism is the disruption of internal balance, countries often utilize discretionary adjustment policies to protect their economies from external forces. Discretionary adjustments mainly consist of expenditure-switching and expenditure-changing policies. The former include altering the exchange rate or, with a fixed exchange rate, varying the relative price level via tariffs, etc., in order to redirect domestic and foreign expenditures between domestic and foreign markets. The latter involve the use of fiscal and monetary policies to change the level of national income and expenditure; included are expenditure-increasing and -reducing measures. Discretionary adjustment policies denote the government's attempt to modify the effects of automatic adjustment in accordance with domestic goals.

Although the process of adjustment is mutual, in that the reallocation of resources is shared by surplus and deficit countries, adjustment costs exist which are not necessarily shared.[8] The first, a permanent cost, occurs after all adjustment has taken place and falls entirely on the deficit nation. Measured in terms of real national absorption forgone, this cost implies that after adjustment is complete the former deficit country will be in a relatively inferior position to the former surplus country. This is because it now receives a smaller share of the combined output of the two nations. This suggests a deterioration in the deficit country's terms of trade in that a given amount of its exports now exchanges in the international market for a smaller quantity of imports.

The second, a transitional cost, is the sacrifice of national income forgone when restoring equilibrium; it is measured by the extent to which disequilibrium countries must permit inflation or unemployed resources, so that mutual equilibrium can be attained. Unlike the permanent cost, the transitional cost implies a problem of distributing the relative burden of adjustment between the surplus and deficit countries. Under the dollar-gold system, lasting from the late 1940s until 1971, asymmetrical adjustments resulted in a deflationary bias. Deficit nations were pressured to adopt deflationary policies, while surplus nations could often forestall adjustment. Although a surplus results in inefficient use of resources in terms of forgone present or future output and welfare, surplus reserves do provide benefits in that they allow a country flexibility in postponing future adjustments. The magnitude of transitional costs has varied greatly since the relative costs of inflating and deflating have differed within and among countries because of differences in economic structures and institutions.

How would the transitional costs of adjustment likely be distributed among nations if the adjustment mechanism is free to operate automatically through variations in relative prices, incomes, and exchange rates? One study suggests that assessing adjustment burdens implies that normative issues relating to economic and political structures and institutions which influence the capacity and desire to avoid adjustment costs must be considered. Highly industrialized, capital-exporting nations with rapidly expanding and diversified economies tend to have sufficient international power to shift the adjustment burden to less developed countries, whose economies are largely capital-importing and geared toward the production of primary goods.[9]

INTERNATIONAL LIQUIDITY

Two incompatible objectives of an international payments mechanism are stability and freedom—stability of exchange rates to encourage international trade and investment, and freedom for nations to pursue their economic objectives without external balance constraints. International reserves—gold, reserve currencies (notably the U.S. dollar and British pound), drawing positions at the IMF, and Special Drawing Rights (SDRs)—are acceptable means of international payments that may be used for the settlement of transactions and defending the value of an exchange rate in times of disequilibrium. International liquidity, a broader concept, refers to international reserves as well as conditional credit facilities such as swap arrangements. Since these terms are highly similar in nature, they will be used interchangeably in this study. The purpose of international liquidity is to render the capacity to weather periods of short-run balance-of-payments disequilibrium without having to resort to undesirable discretionary adjustment policies. When international transactions are kept free from government restrictions, the conflicting aims of stability and freedom may become more harmonized. International liquidity involves dimensions of quantity and quality. Should the growth of liquidity fall short of the rise in the value of international transactions (i.e., quantity), fear of a liquidity crisis may develop. If there exist doubts concerning the value or convertibility of a reserve asset into other assets (i.e., quality), the potential of liquidity to enhance the international monetary mechanism will be limited.

The interrelationship between adjustment and liquidity problems can be illustrated by the use of a diagram.[10] Diagram 2-1 divides the world into two parts—the U.S. and the rest of the world (i.e., ROW), and represents their money incomes on the two axes.

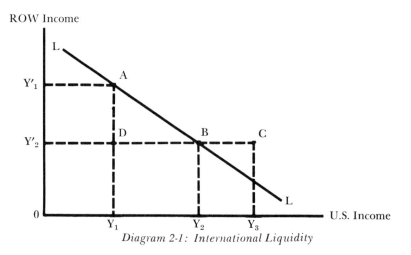

Diagram 2-1: International Liquidity

Line LL is the liquidity balance line. Each point on the line represents an equilibrium combination of ROW and U.S. incomes where the global supply and demand for liquidity equate. To show why LL is downward sloping, assume the U.S. and the

ROW are initially located at an equilibrium point A, where U.S. income is Y_1 and ROW income is Y'_1. Now suppose that U.S. income rises to Y_2. Since the demand for liquidity is a direct function of income, this would induce higher amounts demanded by the U.S. Because the stock of global liquidity is constant along LL, the fulfillment of higher U.S. needs for liquidity requires that ROW income must be smaller, $Y'_2 < Y'_1$.

Any combination of ROW and U.S. incomes that denotes a point to the right of LL signifies a liquidity shortage. Starting from equilibrium point B, suppose the U.S. income expands from Y_2 to Y_3 but ROW income remains constant. A higher global income implies that the global demand for liquidity increases while the supply remains constant—thus a liquidity shortage. Analagously, it can be shown that a point to the left of LL represents a liquidity surplus. Should global liquidity increase, line LL would shift outward to the right; this implies that higher incomes for both the U.S. and the ROW could be maintained by a given amount of liquidity.

Illustrating the adjustment problem, line BB of Diagram 2-2

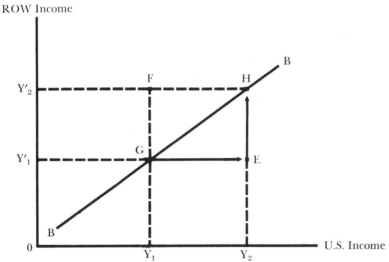

Diagram 2-2: *International Adjustment Mechanism*

represents the mutual external balance positions of the U.S. and the ROW. All points on BB imply that the U.S. and the ROW achieve mutual external balance. At point E, below BB, the U.S.

has a deficit balance-of-payments position due to high income and import levels, while the ROW's low income implies less imports and a balance-of-payments surplus; at point F, above BB, the U.S. experiences surplus and the ROW has deficit payment positions. Line BB is upsloping since a simultaneous improvement in incomes of the two countries can maintain external balance. Assume the initial position is point G; if the U.S. income rises by Y_1-Y_2, while the ROW's income initially remains constant at Y'_1, to attain mutual external balance the ROW's income must rise by Y'_1-Y'_2 to move back to BB.

Diagram 2-3 combines the liquidity and adjustment problems

ROW Income

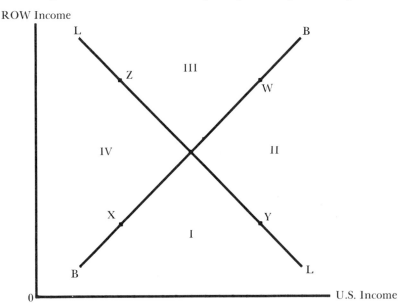

Diagram 2-3: International Liquidity and Adjustment Mechanism

and illustrates the direction of change that enhances mutual external balance and the correct stock of liquidity. Point X denotes surplus liquidity with mutual external balance; the attainment of liquidity balance requires that both countries move toward line LL by expanding their incomes. There is no liquidity problem at point Y, but mutual external balance calls for U.S. deflation and ROW inflation. Similarly, point W implies a liquidity shortage with mutual external equilibrium, while point Z denotes mutual external disequilibrium and the correct stock of liquidity.

Table 2-1 represents four mixed disequilibrium possibilities in which the combination of incomes results in points on neither line LL nor line BB.

Table 2-1: Liquidity and Adjustment Problems

Zones	Liquidity Problem	Adjustment Problem
I	Surplus	U.S. Deficit
II	Shortage	U.S. Deficit
III	Shortage	ROW Deficit
IV	Surplus	ROW Deficit

As will be discussed in Chapter 5, the dollar-gold system did not ensure proper liquidity nor symmetrical adjustment. Prior to 1971 it was generally felt that U.S. deficits were needed to provide sufficient liquidity, and that the U.S. should not be allowed to unilaterally adjust its exchange rate to attain external balance. This suggests that during the late 1960s and early 1970s the U.S. and the ROW were in Zone II of Diagram 2-3 because of the continuous U.S. deficits. This disrupted confidence in the dollar's international value and in the international payments mechanism.

CONFIDENCE PROBLEM

Interest in the confidence problem has been intensified by marked developments since the devaluation of the British pound in 1967: speculative runs on the West German mark, Japan's yen, and other strong currencies in 1971 and 1973; a rising speculative demand for gold that reached a peak in 1974; exchange rate uncertainties between the time of the August, 1971, floating of the U.S. dollar and the December, 1971, Smithsonian Agreements; the 1973 monetary crisis which destroyed the Smithsonian Agreements and resulted in a system of managed floating exchange rates. The confidence problem's existence can be attributed to an international payments mechanism based on more than one reserve asset, and an inadequate functioning of the mechanism that assures unlimited convertibility of reserve assets at a fixed price.[11] There are two explanations of how the confidence problem might arise—a short-run formulation and a long-run formulation. The short-run formulation will first be analyzed.

The short-run formulation deals with the composition of the existing stock of reserve assets.[12] If under a multiple reserve asset system composed of dollars and gold, the U.S. allows its ratio of gold assets to liquid liabilities to fall below acceptable levels, other countries tend to lose confidence in the permanency of the official conversion rate between the dollar and gold, thus encouraging movements out of the reserve asset anticipated to depreciate (i.e., U.S. dollar) and into the reserve asset expected to appreciate (i.e., gold and other hard currencies). Large random shifts among existing reserve assets weaken the system by constraining the adjustment mechanism, imposing pressures upon exchange rates, and disrupting international trade and payments.[13]

In contrast to the first formulation's emphasis upon the fixed stock of reserve assets, the long-run formulation focuses on the process of acquiring additional reserve currencies. If the U.S. supplies additional liquidity through balance-of-payments deficits, its outstanding dollar liabilities expand relative to gold assets. The deterioration of confidence in the ability of the U.S. to maintain unlimited convertibility of its currency into gold suggests foreign reluctance to accept further quantities of dollar liabilities.[14]

The long-run confidence problem is illustrated in Diagram 2-4, which assumes a dollar-gold reserve system.[15] The northeast quadrant represents the international reserve position of countries other than the U.S. (i.e., ROW). According to its desired ratio of international assets, shown by the slope of $(G/d)_1$, the ROW initially holds R_a international reserves, composed of D_1 dollars and G_1 gold. The total monetary stock of world gold is shown in the northwest quadrant; of the initial stock, G_a, the ROW holds G_1 while the U.S. share is G_3. Geometrically, the ROW's G_1 gold stock on the vertical axis equals G_a-G_3 gold stock on the horizontal axis. Representing the reserve position of the U.S., the southwest quadrant shows that the U.S. reserve ratio is shown by the slope of $(G/d)_2$, in which it has G_3 gold and D_1 dollar liabilities. The U.S. reserve position is found geometrically by transferring ROW dollar holdings in the northeast quadrant to the southeast quadrant by way of a 45 degree line.

Now assume that total reserves expand to R_b, where dollar liabilities' growth exceeds the G_b-G_a expansion of world gold stocks.

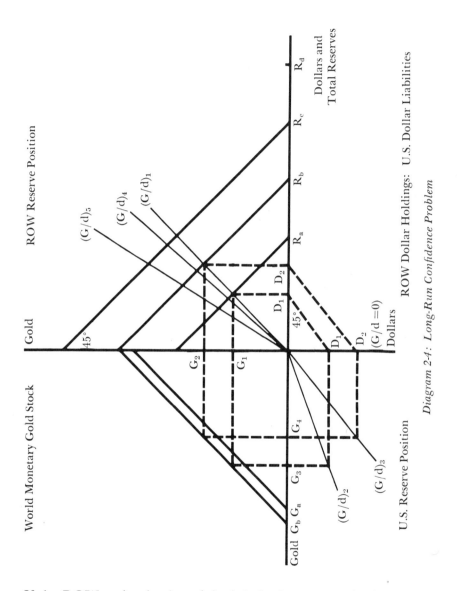

Diagram 2-4: Long-Run Confidence Problem

If the ROW maintains its original desired reserve ratio, its dollar holdings rise to D_2 and its gold holdings increase to G_2; the U.S. gold stocks fall to G_4 and its dollar liabilities rise to D_2, denoting a decline in its reserve ratio, shown by the slope of $(G/d)_3$.

As long as the ROW demand for total reserves expands faster

than the growth of world gold stocks, and the ROW maintains a constant desired ratio of gold to dollars, the reserve position of the U.S. will deteriorate. However, the long-run confidence problem implies that the ROW preference for gold rises relative to dollars as total reserves grow primarily from U.S. deficits. In Diagram 2-4, as total reserves expand to R_c and R_d, the slopes of the ROW desired reserve ratio increase, denoted by $(G/d)_4$ and $(G/d)_5$. Ultimately, foreign dollar holdings tend to reach a limit, whereby subsequent increments of total reserves require increasing world gold stocks or a new form of international reserve asset.

INTERDEPENDENCE OF INTERNATIONAL ADJUSTMENT, LIQUIDITY, AND CONFIDENCE

Two broad categories of actions for coping with deficits in payment balances under a system of pegged exchange rates are discretionary adjustment measures, including expenditure-reducing and expenditure-switching policies, and the use of available liquidity for financing payment imbalances.

Diagram 2-5 illustrates these policy alternatives by use of a triangle, of which the area represents the magnitude of disequilibrium and the vertices signify the exclusive use of each of the policy alternatives.[16] Each point within the triangle refers to some combination of the three policies for achieving internal and external balance; the closer a point is to a vertex, the greater is the reliance on that policy.

The diagram suggests that several propositions must be considered in forming economic policy. First, it is necessary to consider the financial strength of the deficit country and the time period involved; if the deficit is viewed to be short-term, or the deficit country has large stocks of international reserves, the immediate pressure on that country to adjust would likely be relatively small. Second, one cannot designate independently the objectives and effects of the three policy alternatives on an economy, for they may result in differing consequences for external and internal balance. For instance, the use of international liquidity is relevant for short-run imbalances, while in the case of long-run adjustment for large diversified economies with small foreign trade sectors, the costs of expenditure reduction are more than that of expenditure switching.[17] Third, the preferred policy

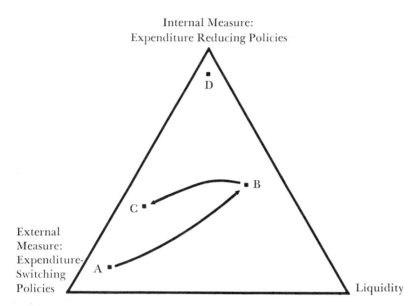

Internal Measure:
Expenditure Reducing Policies

External
Measure:
Expenditure-
Switching
Policies

Liquidity

Diagram 2-5: Interdependence of International Adjustment, Liquidity,
and Confidence

mix is largely a political choice, for it depends on dimensions of ideology, such as a planned versus a laissez-faire economy and the degree of mutual confidence in the ability of nations to practice financial discipline.

For the above reasons, most nations historically have avoided extreme forms of these policy alternatives. From the early post–World War II years until 1971, the dollar-gold system evolved away from reliance on extreme external measures such as exchange controls and import quotas, and toward greater use of internal adjustments and international liquidity, suggesting a movement from point A toward point B in diagram 2-5.[18] However, the U.S. decisions to float the dollar in 1971 and devalue the dollar in 1971 and 1973, and the system of floating exchange rates adopted by many nations after the 1973 termination of the Smithsonian Agreements exemplify a movement toward greater use of external policies, implying a shift from point B toward point C.

This chapter has presented an overview of the problems relating to the IMF system—liquidity, adjustment, and confidence. Because these areas of difficulty are chief concerns of any monetary authority, they will be used throughout this study as a means of evaluating alternative monetary systems and reform proposals. As will later be discussed, there also exists a global problem involving the distribution of liquidity among the advanced and less developed countries. Because the less developed countries require large amounts of capital for development purposes, and since they generally must face balance-of-payments deficits to finance capital investments, their need for liquidity is great. Developmental assistance has been and will continue to be considered an important issue relating to international monetary reform.

CHAPTER 3

The Nature of International Liquidity

INTRODUCTION

This chapter analyzes the nature of international liquidity by considering its purpose, sources of demand and supply, and problems.

As mentioned in the previous chapter, when under a system of pegged exchange rates a nation's autonomous international payments exceed its autonomous international receipts, some form of settlement is required to finance the ensuing deficit. International liquidity enables countries to maintain stable exchange rates and weather periods of short-term external deficits without having to resort to undesirable corrective measures—restrictions on international transactions, unnecessarily severe domestic deflationary policies, etc. Acting as a buffer, liquidity assists the attaining of domestic economic objectives by permitting monetary authorities more time to initiate desirable adjustment policies. However, because a country's stock of liquidity is limited, its ability to finance deficit balances is temporary.

SOURCES OF INTERNATIONAL LIQUIDITY

The dollar-gold system's emphasis upon freedom of international trade and payments and exchange-rate stability required

17

that deficit nations transfer an acceptable means of settlement to their creditors, which could take the forms of owned and borrowed reserves. Owned reserves, including gold, reserve currencies, and Special Drawing Rights (i.e., SDRs), are chiefly accumulated by a nation's ability to maintain a surplus in its balance of payments. However, just as an effective adjustment mechanism may reduce the need for owned reserves, so can a nation's capacity to borrow to finance payment imbalances. A country's international reserve position is composed of owned reserves and borrowed reserves which include drawing positions at the IMF and other conditional credit facilities such as swap arrangements.[1]

Gold. Of the several forms of international liquidity, gold historically has played the dominant role in terms of asset quality and prestige. Table 3-1 suggests that although gold as a propor-

Table 3-1: Composition of IMF Countries' Reserves (Percent)

	1950	1960	1970	1971	1972
Gold	69.0	61.1	40.4	29.7	24.8
SDRs	----	----	3.4	4.8	6.0
Reserve positions in the IMF	3.4	5.8	8.4	5.2	4.4
Foreign Exchange	27.6	33.1	47.8	60.3	64.8
Total	100.0	100.0	100.0	100.0	100.0

Data: *IMF Survey* (September 10, 1973), p. 262.

tion of total monetary reserves has declined from 69 percent in 1950 to 24.8 percent in 1972, it still exerts significant influence in the international monetary system. The supply of gold as a reserve asset depends not only upon production, but also upon the quantities supplied and absorbed by nonmonetary uses. Of the total stock of world gold, worth roughly $109 billion, it is estimated that the amount held for monetary uses constitutes 46 percent, while 54 percent is in private hands, used for art objects and jewelry, coins and bars, and industrial purposes.[2]

The quantities of gold supplied, of which South Africa produces at least two-thirds of the world's total, primarily depend upon their prices.[3] Until 1968 the price of gold was kept near $35 per ounce due to the U.S. commitment to transact unlimited quantities with foreign governments, and the practice of monetary authorities taking all the gold off the market not bought by private buyers. As will be discussed in Chapter 5, in March, 1968, a "two-tier" policy was adopted in which international supply and demand determined the free market price of gold, while the central banks maintained an official price of $35 per ounce.

As a source of reserve assets, the growth of gold has not kept pace with the expansion of international transactions. From the early 1960s through 1972 the volume of world trade grew by an average annual rate of 8 percent; although world gold production (see Table 3-2) grew by nearly 11 percent from 1962 to 1970, less

Table 3-2: World Gold Production, 1962–1970 (in Millions of U.S. Dollars at $35 per Fine Ounce)

		Annual Data or Annual Average Rates			
	1962	*1964*	*1966*	*1968*	*1970*
South Africa	892.2	1,018.9	1,080.8	1,088.0	1,128.0
Canada	145.5	133.0	114.6	94.1	84.3
United States	54.5	51.4	63.1	53.9	63.5
Other Africa	64.4	64.7	54.2	55.6	51.1
Latin America	44.9	41.9	38.6	33.1	31.9
Asia	40.3	40.1	43.6	47.1	52.3
Europe	15.0	15.1	12.6	11.1	8.6
Oceania	42.7	39.4	37.2	32.4	26.7
World Total	1,299.5	1,404.5	1,444.7	1,415.3	1,446.4

Data: *International Financial Statistics* (December, 1973), p. 17.

than half of that was used for international reserves.[4] The adoption of other forms of reserve assets stems from the shortage of gold supplied for monetary uses at the official price.

Reserve Currencies. The major source of international liquidity is the supply of foreign currencies, notably the U.S. dollar and British pound. Table 3-1 shows that as a component of IMF country reserves, the stock of foreign exchange increased from 27.6 percent in 1950 to 64.9 percent in 1972. These currencies, referred to as reserve currencies, or sometimes as key currencies, derive their significance in that nations generally have been willing to hold them as a form of reserves. Since the August, 1971, U.S. suspension of the convertibility of the dollar into gold, its function as a reserve currency no longer exists. In defining a reserve currency, three interdependent characteristics can be identified—

media of settlement, source of liquidity, and agent of intervention.[5]

For international transactions, traders select a currency in which their settlements are conducted. To fulfill the role of a transaction currency, the currency in question must first hold a leading position in the international monetary system. During the 1880–1914 era, the British pound was the leading currency since London was the commercial and financial capital of the world, accounting for some 40 percent of trade in manufactured products; since World War II, the U.S. dollar has maintained a leading position among the world's major currencies. Traders must also feel confident in the stability of a currency's purchasing power relative to other currencies. And last, there must be confidence that the currency can be converted at a fixed price into another reserve asset (i.e., gold); a major responsibility of the monetary authorities of a transaction currency nation is to practice financial discipline to ensure their currency's convertibility.

Another characteristic is that not only must a reserve currency be freely convertible into other reserve assets, but that it must also supply the world with an adequate stock of liquidity. However, this role may be inconsistent in the long run with the transaction function. As will be explained in Chapter 5, a successful operation of the dollar-gold system required full confidence in the quality of reserve assets; the act of supplying additional liquidity via payments deficits of the reserve centers often undermined the confidence in their currencies' values.

When central banks operate in the foreign exchange markets, they use currencies which fulfill an intervention role. To qualify as an intervention currency, as asset must be widely accepted throughout the world as a means of settlement, must maintain world confidence in its function as a reserve asset, and must be fully convertible upon demand into gold and other currencies at a fixed price. Prior to the advent of the dollar-gold system, international settlements were made in gold; since any intervention in the foreign exchange market implied the use of whatever currency occupied the strongest position at that time, there existed no intervention currencies in the present form. Contrary to the original intentions of the dollar-gold system, which envisioned the pre–World War II practice of member countries directly intervening in the foreign exchange markets, a fully convertible dollar, in the asset and market sense, became the intervention currency; it was not until the 1958 restoration of European market convertibility that the pound also regained prominence as an intervention currency.[6] There are two forms of currency convertibility, market and asset. Market convertibility means that any holder of a currency, say the U.S. dollar, can use it not only to buy and invest in the U.S., but also to convert his dollars into other currency in the market at the prevailing exchange rate. Asset convertibility, which applied exclusively to the U.S. under the dollar-gold system, implied that the dollar was convertible into any U.S. reserve asset, notably gold.

IMF Drawing Facilities. Besides serving as a medium of international settlement, reserves can be used to support the par values of currencies in times of short-term payments disequilibrium. The IMF stands ready to provide short-term credits, known as drawing positions, to deficit member nations whose reserves are insufficient to maintain stable exchange rates.

Each member country is assigned a quota, which determines its voting power, drawing rights, and the amount of its subscription contributed to the Fund. The size of a country's quota is governed by such factors as its volume of foreign trade, national income, international reserves, and the size of its exports relative to national income. A quota normally consists of 25 percent in gold, known as the gold tranche, and 75 percent in national currencies. The amount of gold a nation must contribute equals 25 percent of its quota, or 10 percent of its international gold and dollar reserves, whichever is smaller.

When a deficit nation requires short-term credit, it can borrow the foreign currency it needs by depositing an equivalent amount of its own currency with the Fund. A drawing on the Fund changes a quota's composition—the gold tranche portion declines while the currency share increases. Countries whose currencies are being drawn by other nations find their gold tranche increasing. Borrowing from the IMF thus increases total world reserves—the drawing country's level of reserves do not change since the decline in its gold tranche is exactly offset by the rise in currency reserves, but the country whose reserves are being borrowed receives an increase in its gold tranche, and thus in its reserves.

In obtaining loans, a deficit country can automatically draw an amount of foreign currency equal to its gold tranche position.

Conditional drawings beyond the gold tranche are also allowed, carried on under the credit tranche; the maximum limit on drawings occurs when the Fund's holdings of the borrowing country's currency equal 200 percent of its quota. The following example illustrates this point.[7]

Assume that a country has a quota of $2 billion, that it has no Fund drawings, and that no country has drawn its currency. Its reserve position is shown below:

Currency	$1,500 million
Gold	500 million
Gold tranche	(500 million)

If the country borrowed $500 million from the Fund, its gold tranche would be reduced to zero. Hence, the Fund's holdings of its currency would equal $2 billion. The country could then conditionally draw an additional $2 billion before the Fund's holdings of its currency reach 200 percent of its quota. In practice, drawings up to the amount of the credit tranche generally are favorably recognized when the drawings or stand-by arrangements are intended to support a sound program aimed at establishing or maintaining the enduring stability of a member's currency at a realistic rate of exchange.[8]

Special Drawing Rights. IMF drawing facilities do not ensure consistent supplies of international reserves since, as the borrowings are repaid, the level of liquidity also decreases. As a means of increasing the flexibility of the international monetary system, by extending the Fund's automatic drawing rights SDRs have become firmly established as supplements to other reserve assets.[9] In 1969 the IMF approved a proposal that would create a special Fund quota, consisting of approximately SDR 9.5 billion. (In the first allocation of SDRs, the basic period was three years. Subsequent basic periods will likely range from three to five years.) In the first distribution period, 1970–72, these reserve units were allocated in proportion to the 104 participating countries' Fund quotas; of this, the U.S. received about 25 percent, while 64 percent accrued to the major industrial nations combined. Carried out under a special account, SDRs pay to their official holders an annual interest rate of 5 percent on the net holdings—that is, the amount by which a country's SDR holdings exceed its allocation as determined by its IMF quota. SDRs cannot be directly used in making settlements since transactions among participating governments are restricted to the exchange of SDRs for foreign exchange.

The objective behind the SDR creation is to provide a source of owned, not borrowed, reserves. SDRs differ from other reserve assets in the following ways. First, they are a fiduciary (a term which suggests that the SDR does not have any intrinsic value, nor is it redeemable in anything that has) asset designated as a legal means of international settlement, whereas the status of reserve currencies and gold is based primarily on tradition.[10] Second, unlike Fund drawings which must be repaid within three to five years, SDRs are unconditionally owned by the participating country. However, they are restricted strictly to balance-of-payments purposes rather than for altering the composition of a country's reserves or for enhancing a country's external purchasing ability (i.e., developmental assistance). Third, it is expected that a participant's average holding of SDRs should, over time, be at a level above 30 percent of the average amounts it has been allocated. Last, there exists a designation principle whereby participating countries with relatively strong balance-of-payments and reserve positions are required to convert their currency into SDRs upon request of foreign governments. However, the designated countries are not required to accept SDRs once their SDR balance reaches 300 percent of their initial allocations.

When the SDR was first adopted, it was agreed to have its value maintain a fixed tie to the U.S. dollar's par value. This was because the dollar was the key currency of the international monetary system. Not only did all other countries define their currencies' values in terms of the dollar, but the dollar also served as a primary reserve asset. However, this rigid tie between the par value of the dollar and SDR became unacceptable as the result of several monetary developments. First, the 1971 termination of U.S. gold convertibility to foreign governments raised questions concerning whether the gold value of the dollar was sufficiently meaningful for the SDR to bear a fixed tie to the dollar. A second problem resulted from the 1973 adoption of managed floating exchange rates by the major industrialized nations. As a result of the generalized floating, it became possible for the SDR's value to fluctuate against other currencies, while remaining fixed in relation to the dollar. It was primarly because of these problems that in 1974 a new method of SDR valuation was adopted—the basket valuation.

Under the basket valuation approach, the SDR's value is set equal in value to a basket of sixteen world currencies. The result is that the SDR's value is tied to a weighted average of those currencies in the basket. The weighted shares for the sixteen leading currencies, in percents, are: U.S. dollar, 33.0; Deutsche mark, 12.5; pound sterling, 9.0; French franc, 7.5; Japanese yen, 7.5; Canadian dollar, 6.0; Italian lira, 6.0; Netherlands guilder, 4.5; Belgian franc, 3.5; Swedish krona, 2.5; Australian dollar, 1.5; Spanish peseta, 1.5; Norwegian krone, 1.5; Danish krone, 1.5; Austrian schilling, 1.0; South African rand, 1.0.[11] Should the basket currencies appreciate-depreciate in the exchange markets relative to each other, the SDR's value will remain in the center— it would appreciate relative to those currencies floating downward, while depreciating relative to those floating upward. The major advantage of this approach is that the purchasing power of the SDR is independent from exchange rate movements. The SDR would be regarded as a safer asset than a reserve currency (i.e., U.S. dollar) in that it cannot be devalued at the option of any single government.

Other Credit Facilities. Besides official reserves, there are other forms of credit which enhance the liquidity and flexibility of the international payments system. Among these are stand-by credits, General Arrangements to Borrow, and swap arrangements.

There are times when a country may wish to be certain that it can obtain loans from the Fund, but yet it does not require liquidity immediately. Under stand-by credits, the Fund agrees to sell currencies to deficit countries, up to a maximum amount and within a stipulated period, should the need arise. Stand-by credits have frequently been negotiated when a nation's currency is under speculative attack.

Another short-term source of credit is the General Arrangements to Borrow (i.e., GAB), instituted in 1962 by the IMF and its ten major members, the Group of Ten. Due to the possibility that Fund sources of reserve currencies might be exhausted by large drawings, the Fund made arrangements to make loans to deficit nations by first borrowing from major industrial countries; these loans aggregated to $6 billion at the par values in effect at the time the arrangements were made. Thus the IMF serves as a financial intermediary. Such facilities do not constitute a permanent source of international liquidity, for as borrowings are repaid world reserves revert back to their original levels.

The 1958 establishment of market convertibility of all the major European currencies, and the subsequent rise of short-term capital movements during the early 1960s resulted in the IMF's 1962 adoption of reciprocal currency arrangements, commonly called swap arrangements.[12] Among the swap arrangements' objectives are to enhance the stability of the foreign exchange markets and to provide a supplement to drawings made through the IMF.

Under the swap network, bilateral stand-by credit arrangements normally exist between the U.S. and several other countries, the purpose being to provide short-term loans at guaranteed exchange rates. Although swaps are not intended to finance balance-of-payments deficits, they can help discourage destabilizing speculation and attacks on unsound currencies. In July, 1973, the U.S. swap credits with other central banks were increased 50 percent, to approximately $18 billion.[13]

THE DEMAND FOR INTERNATIONAL RESERVES

On a global basis the demand, or need, for international reserves is determined at that point where the effects of further reserve growth on world economic welfare cease to become positive and begin to become negative. Although countries' balance-of-payment positions are interdependent, in the sense that a surplus in one country is matched by a deficit in another, for two reasons the world's demand for reserves cannot be calculated by adding up the demands of single countries.

First, through policy coordination countries may improve the adjustment mechanism, hence reducing payments disequilibrium and the need for reserves. Diagram 3-1 dynamically illustrates this point for a single nation.[14]

In the upper part of Diagram 3-1, curve A is based on the assumption that no favorable policy coordination nor adjustments occur. The surplus and deficit payments for curve A are measured by the area between the horizontal axis and the curve. With no policy coordination, curve A suggests relatively large external disequilibriums as well as no significant reductions in the range of disequilibriums over time. In like manner, curve B illustrates the magnitude of payments imbalances. However, two notable differences exist: (1) the disequilibrium regions under curve B

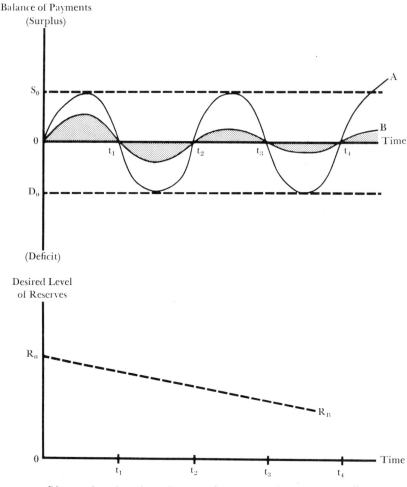

Diagram 3-1: *Interdependence of the Need for Reserves and Policy Coordination*

are less than that of curve A; (2) the range of curve B's payments imbalances declines over time. This is because curve B reflects the assumption that, over time, policy coordination results in a more efficient adjustment mechanism which reduces the range of fluctuations of balance-of-payments disequilibriums, thus reducing the needed reserves. If inadequate policy measures or improperly timed ones are utilized, curve B could shift outside curve A, resulting in a larger preferred level of reserves.

The lower part of Diagram 3-1 illustrates how a single nation's external imbalances can affect its preferred level of reserves. Curve R_B has been arbitrarily started at point R_0, the point of the country's desired reserve position without policy coordination. This point implies that the country feels it must have R_0 reserves to finance any worst-possible anticipated deficit. The time path of curve R_B reflects that followed by curve B, which assumes an ever-improving adjustment mechanism. Because of the smaller and smaller fluctuations in the balance-of-payments disequilibriums, curve R_B declines over time. This suggests that the preferred reserve level expected to meet any potential payments deficit decreases. Diagram 3-1 thus concludes that as a nation confidently anticipates a successful reduction in its payments disequilibriums its desired level of reserves will decrease.

There is a second reason why the world's demand for reserves cannot be calculated simply by adding up the demands of single countries. Because the quantity and quality of reserves can influence the burden of adjustment between surplus and deficit countries, the stock of reserves accessible to a country may affect the economic policies of others. A political question arises as to what constitutes an adequate level of reserves and degree of freedom in managing an economy. Since the benefits and costs of reserves are generally not equal for surplus and deficit countries, they are likely to disagree on world reserve levels, thus restricting the precision of reserve determination.[15]

In assessing the need for reserves, the efficacy of the adjustment mechanism must be considered. Not all forms of adjustment improvements necessarily reduce the demand for reserves. Effective income policies, exchange rate policies, and aggregate spending policies would tend to reduce the demand for reserves. Although restrictions on trade and investment might improve the adjustment mechanism, they could also intensify the need for reserves.[16] First, the speed of adjustment may be affected by the quantity of reserves; countries with negligible supplies might be forced to adjust quickly, while those with large quantities may postpone adjustment indefinitely. Second, for countries with surplus payment positions, there tends to be a direct relation between the efficacy of the adjustment mechanism and the need for reserves. If adjustment is allowed to operate, surpluses tend to decrease while the need for reserves tends to increase. Third, for deficit countries the relationship between the need for reserves and the adjustment mechanism is likely to be the opposite, for in the short run, reserves help insulate deficit countries' internal balances from external forces.

Diagram 3-2 illustrates the efficacy of the adjustment mechanism in context of the degree of exchange rate flexibility.[17] Assuming the normal shapes of the demand and supply curves of foreign

Exchange Rate

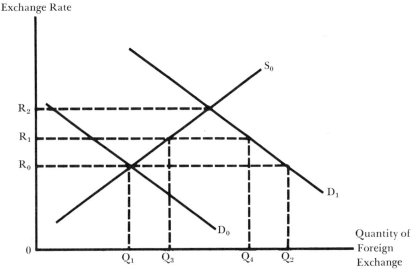

Diagram 3-2: Exchange Rate Flexibility and the Demand for International Reserves

exchange (which implies that the elasticity of demand for foreign exchange is greater than zero and less than infinite, and that the foreign demand for domestic exports is elastic), suppose a country's imports increase, resulting in a rise in its demand for foreign exchange from D_0 to D_1. If this deficit country maintains a fixed rate of exchange at R_0, it will require Q_1-Q_2 units of foreign reserves to settle the deficit. If bands are adopted, such as those of the Smithsonian Agreements, the country's exchange rate might automatically depreciate to the outer limit of the band, say R_1, before necessitating a need for foreign reserves of Q_3-Q_4. However, if exchange rates are allowed to float freely, an automatic depreciation to R_2 would ensure equilibrium at which there would exist no need for reserves. The implication is that for deficit nations there tends to exist an inverse relationship between the need for reserves and the degree of exchange rate flexibility.

Diagram 3-3 conceptually illustrates the relationship between the need for reserves and the degree of exchange rate flexibility.[18]

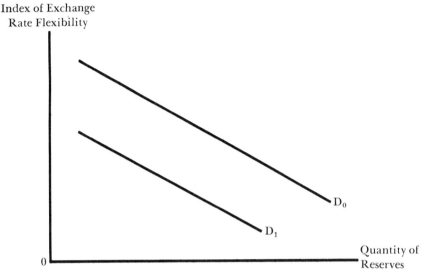

Diagram 3-3: *Aggregate World Reserves Demanded*

The conceptual index of exchange rate flexibility on the vertical axis suggests the importance of this variable as a determinant of the need (i.e., demand) for reserves. An empirical formulation of this index would involve an ex-post measurement of exchange rate variations that have occurred in some stipulated period, and the size of the involved country's foreign trade sector. Zero flexibility in the index would imply completely fixed exchange rates, while an index value of one suggests a system of freely floating exchange rates. The demand for reserves is downsloping, conceptually reflecting the inverse relationship between the need for reserves and the degree of exchange rate flexibility. Shifts in the demand for reserves are determined by the following economic factors.[19]

A major objective determinant of the demand for reserves is the capacity and willingness of a country to undergo domestic adjustments. *Ceteris paribus,* the greater a country's propensity to use expenditure-changing measures or forms of expenditure-switching policies other than exchange rate variations that effectively counteract external balance disequilibrium, the smaller will be the need for reserves. Curve D_0 of Diagram 3-3 thus moves leftward toward the origin. As will be later discussed, at the September, 1973, IMF meetings on international monetary reform, the U.S. proposed to improve the adjustment mechanism by adopting the following plan—as payment surpluses grow too fast, measured by an objective indicator of changes in central bank reserves, the offending nation must justify to the Fund why it is not reducing its surpluses. Although these rules would not rigidly force surplus countries to comply, they would attempt to "persuade" countries to voluntarily adhere to the plan.

International coordination of economic policies is another objective determinant. Diagram 3-1 implies that if international cooperation can reduce the frequency and severity of payments imbalances, the need for reserves will be reduced. A primary goal of the European Economic Community's pursuit of a full monetary union is the adoption of a common macroeconomic policy in which there would be liberal capital movements and a single currency. Other things being equal, such an integration of monetary and fiscal policies would likely lessen the demand for international reserves, hence shifting D_0 to the left. Should the European Economic Community become a "single country" and have one currency, the flexibility needed to adjust any imbalance becomes zero. This limiting case implies that the demand for reserves would move leftward until it reached the origin.

As shown by the international monetary crises of 1968, 1971, and 1973, the rise of destabilizing short-term capital flows has disrupted the operation of and confidence in the international payments mechanism. Central banks, largely influenced by a precautionary motive for holding reserves, anticipate rising needs for liquidity in time of crisis, causing the demand for reserves to shift outward to the right. Central bank cooperation, in the forms of swap arrangements, etc., can influence the need for reserves. To the extent that cooperation restores confidence in the system, it may reduce the magnitude and duration of destabilizing forces, thus shifting the demand for reserves to the left.

Another objective determinant relates to the quality of a reserve asset and the benefits it generates. Because it costs a country to hold reserves in the form of forgone consumption and investment, a country must consider the advantages of holding reserves. These benefits mainly arise from the fact that reserves provide governments the capacity to intervene in foreign exchange markets and temporarily cushion their internal balances from external disturbances. In weighing the marginal benefits against costs, the quality of the reserve asset must be considered. For instance, if a reserve currency is viewed unsound, fear of capital losses may result in a movement out of that asset before its anticipated devaluation occurs. The international monetary crisis of 1973 saw a massive flight out of the dollar into the mark and yen, which were expected to appreciate in value. The point is that, *ceteris paribus,* the greater the quality and anticipated rate of return of holding a reserve asset, the greater will be its demand.

Other objective determinants concern the level of global prices and real income. The need for reserves relates both to the frequency of imbalances in international transactions and the market value of these imbalances. A general rise in the world price level tends to increase the demand for reserves. Assuming constant world prices, growth in the level of global real income also tends to increase the need for reserves.

Assessing Reserve Adequacy—Statement of Issues

The behavior of the dollar-gold standard implies the involvement of four interdependent dimensions, when one ascertains whether a given stock of reserves is adequate to enhance the objectives of the international payments mechanism.[20]

Short-Term Adequacy. Under a system of pegged exchange rates, the adequacy of reserves depends largely upon the objective economic factors relating to the magnitude, duration, and frequency of the temporary payments disequilibrium. There is no way to measure reserve adequacy, because there are also subjective, political-economic factors requiring normative judgments which determine the need for reserves.[21] For instance, reserve adequacy can only be defined with respect to national objectives; other things being equal, a country pursuing noninflationary full employment at the cost of external imbalance would likely require a greater stock of international reserves than one permitting more flexible internal and external adjustments.

Short-term reserve adequacy can be analyzed only in the context of the geographical unit to which the problem applies. For a single nation, the adequacy of reserves relates to the objective and subjective criteria in conjunction with national goals. Although global reserve adequacy essentially reduces itself to the determination of reserve adequacy of individual countries, the global approach also includes a distribution problem. Adequate quantities of global reserves misallocated among surplus and deficit countries may lead to liquidity crises and costly asymmetrical adjustments. Assessing global reserve adequacy thus entails a normative judgment of whether the world's reserves and resources are reasonably allocated. A related problem involves the distribution of reserves among the industrially advanced and less developed countries. The term reserve adequacy best applies to advanced nations since it relates to the short-run question of financing payment imbalances, etc. Less developed countries normally face liquidity shortages, for in addition to financing short-term deficits they require reserves for the financing of long-term development programs.[22] However, oil-producing Arab countries have experienced surplus reserves, because the revenues from their oil exports have exceeded the costs of financing industrialization.

Flexibility. Another issue involved in assessing reserve adequacy is the flexibility of reserves. Basically a short-term issue, it is a problem of quality rather than quantity. Not only must there be adequate quantities of reserve assets, but they must also be sufficiently mobile and liquid to respond rapidly to disequilibriums and/or speculative crises. The dimension of flexibility is normally associated with reserve center countries, for it is their liabilities that may undermine confidence in the stability and efficacy of the payments mechanism.

Long-Run Adequacy. The issue of long-run adequacy, or expansibility, concerns the future supplies of reserves relative to their need for financing international transactions and long-term capital flows. Among the reasons why the secular need for reserves tends to grow are: as the world economy expands, so do prices of raw materials and the value of international transactions; the goals of economic development and full employment generally require expanding levels of reserves for the less developed and the advanced countries.[23] Reserve expansibility relates to the problem of long-run confidence, discussed in Chapter 2—under a multicurrency reserve system, expanding currency assets imply the need to maintain market convertibility to ensure confidence; if gold is included as a reserve asset, full confidence in the currency assets necessitates the need for asset convertibility.

Diagram 3-4 conceptally illustrates the political-economic

problem of assessing a long-run range of reserve adequacy for a single country. The upper limit of the range, shown by line UU, is determined by objective and subjective factors relating to the political and economic costs of holding reserves, which include potential inflation and forgone consumption and investment. The

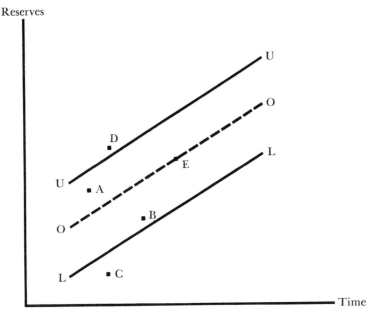

Diagram 3-4: Long-Run Reserve Adequacy and Optimality for a Single Country

range's lower limit, shown by line LL, is determined by economic and political dimensions involving potential losses of convertibility, disruptions of international transactions and payments, high unemployment levels, etc. Both the upper and lower boundaries are upwardsloping since they reflect the previously mentioned tendency for an upward secular demand for reserves. At any given moment, a country's stock of reserves may fall within lines UU and LL, such as points A or B, indicating that the existing quantity of reserves reasonably enhances a country's objectives. However, the undesirable points C and D indicate deficient and excessive quantities of reserves respectively, implying the need for internal and/or external adjustments and the readjustment in official reserve positions.

Reserve Optimality. Conceptually at each point in time and within the range of long-run reserve adequacy there is some precise quantity of reserves at which the benefits of higher employment and reduced impediments to international transactions equal the costs of inflation and recourse to official compensatory financing. In objective terms, the optimal level of reserves is given by that quantity which minimizes the total cost of adjusting and/or financing an external imbalance.[24] There is only one level of adequate reserves which is also optimal in the sense that, at this level, world welfare is maximized and adjustment policies are the most efficient.[25] However, since a definition of optimal reserves must also include subjective criteria, any quantitative measurement of optimal reserves is imprecise. Diagram 3-4 conceptually suggests in qualitative terms that within the range denoted by lines UU and LL there is at each moment in time some level of optimal reserves, shown by any point on line OO, that uniquely enhances global welfare and adjustments. Several writers have attempted to describe in quantitative and qualitative terms the nature of optimal reserves.[26]

A quantitative measure of optimal reserves for a single country is calculated by H. R. Heller, who uses a comparative cost-benefit approach in which the cost equals the opportunity cost of holding reserves, while the benefit refers to the avoidance of adjustments for combating external deficits.[27] Heller determines a level of optimal reserves by calculating the probability that a deficit country will run out of reserves. He next compares actual reserves with his measure of optimal reserves to establish empirical conclusions. A basic conclusion of his analysis is that the advanced countries which are not reserve centers generally have excess reserves, while the less developed countries have less than optimal reserves.

A basic assumption of the quantitative measures of reserve adequacy is that reserves are held to meet random and/or systematic drains associated with varying flows of current account payments and receipts. However, these measures are of limited validity for two reasons. First, destabilizing speculation results in uncertainty, since capital flows tend to involve a psychological battle of nerves, wit, and bluff, far outside the realm of objective economic criteria.[28] Second, government motivations and value judgments concerning the relative importance of economic goals often differ, implying that subjective factors also explain the need for reserves.

A qualitative approach in developing a theoretically determinable level of optimum reserves for a single country is used by T. Balogh.[29] Taking a long-run view, Balogh assumes that economic growth is an integral part of policy, and emphasizes the opportunity cost of holding reserves. Reserve growth is optimal if it promotes a maximum rate of economic expansion, given the existing stock of resources and level of saving. A country should accumulate reserves only if they promote increasing investment in the long run. A major limitation of Balogh's approach is that it applies mainly to the growth oriented, less developed countries, having less relevance for industrially advanced countries.

In contrast to Balogh, J. M. Flemming utilizes a conceptual model that determines an optimal rate of reserve accumulation for industrially advanced countries.[30] Flemming considers reserve stocks and growth rates to be optimal if they maximize the degree of reserve ease, which is the extent to which authorities are confident in their ability to use reserves to finance payment deficits without resorting to expenditure-changing and/or expenditure-switching policies.

The upper part of Diagram 3-5 illustrates the static relationship between reserve stocks and reserve growth rates for a single country by use of an indifference map, whose contours represent degrees of central bankers' confidence that their reserves are sufficient to maintain a given external balance position. Each indifference contour slopes downward, convex to the origin, reflecting the assumptions that the stock and growth rate of reserves are imperfect substitutes in contributing to reserve ease, and that there is a diminishing marginal rate of substitution between the stock and growth rate of reserves. There is also assumed to be some minimum stock of reserves below which reserves must not fall if central bankers' confidence in their reserves is to exist; the indifference contours tend to approach the horizontal as they near this level.

Using a family of reserve paths—denoted by A', B', and C'—the lower part of Diagram 3-5 conceptually illustrates the required, not actual, development in reserves that must take place over time if a given level of confidence in maintaining an external balance position is not to be disturbed. Reserve paths A', B', and C' re-

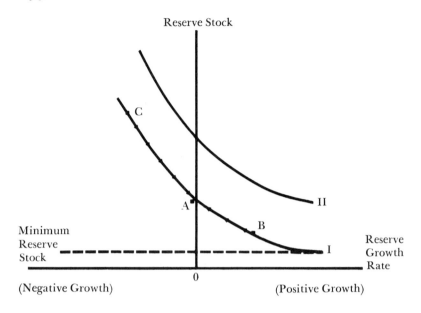

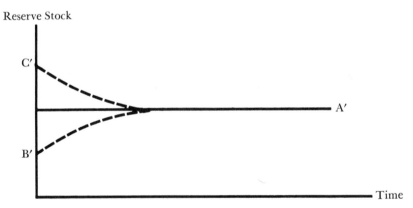

Diagram 3-5: Static Relation of Optimal Reserves and Reserve Ease for a Single Country

spectively correspond to points A, B, and C in the upper part of the diagram.

At time period zero, if a given reserve stock, shown by A, corresponds to point A', there is no need to alter the quantities of reserves over time, for they are optimal. At any initial stock of reserves lower than A, say point B, a positive rate of reserve growth is required to maintain constant levels of confidence; however, the marginal rate of reserve growth will decline, shown by reserve path B' which asymptotically approaches A'. Similarly, if an initial reserve stock, say C, is higher than A, it must fall; this is shown by reserve path C' asymptotically approaching A'. The conclusion is that A' represents an equilibrium level of required reserves in relation to a given external balance position and level of reserve ease—it is the stock of optimal reserves.

IMF Methods of Appraising the Adequacy of Reserves

In assessing the need for reserves, the IMF has used several objective indicators for signaling reserve inadequacy.[31] First, excessive interest rates in the domestic economy—such high levels signify a desire to protect reserve balances by discouraging capital outflows and encouraging capital inflows. Second, intensification of restrictions on international transactions—although it recognizes that these restrictions may be influenced by other factors than global reserves, the Fund holds that world reserve inadequacy may partly necessitate restrictions on trade and capital movements. Third, the act of making the accumulation of reserves an overriding objective of economic policy—this mercantilistic view may likely conflict with other fundamental objectives, such as economic growth, high levels of employment, and freedom of international transactions. Fourth, a persistent instability of exchange rates—such activity is considered a significant symptom of strain, for it may reflect the failure to exercise proper control over internal and external balance. Fifth, the composition of reserve increments—although the decline of reserve growth from traditional sources and the expansion of reserves from use of credit facilities such as Fund credit tranches do not explicitly indicate a decline in reserve adequacy, the Fund generally associates such developments with the need for unconditional international liquidity. The Fund rejects inflation and demand pressure as primary indicators on the grounds that reserves have become a less important determinant of demand policies; also, the operation of the adjustment mechanism is generally not considered a good indicator of reserve adequacy, although it could be in some instances.[32]

Besides having objective indicators of reserve inadequacy, the IMF has utilized several quantitative methods of appraising the adequacy of reserves. Among these are past trends of actual reserves, past ratios of reserves to imports, and past ratios of reserves to the trend of aggregate imbalances. A major problem of these ex-post indicators is that

> the variables neither directly represent the variables that reserve policy is intended to influence nor have a known relationship to them. None is intended to be associated with reserve adequacy, or with any of the components of that heterogeneous target variable. The use of trends in past relationships to project future needs assumes that reserves were adequate in the past period over which the trend is fitted—not in every year, but on the average. It is not possible to tell, from this method, whether there was a trend in the degree of reserve adequacy itself, or if there was, to allow for it quantitatively.[33]

Another limitation is that the Fund's quantitative methods only include objective variables, not recognizing subjective factors. Until a more comprehensive quantitative measure of adequacy is developed, it will be necessary to make qualitative judgments of reserve adequacy.[34]

This chapter has analyzed the nature of liquidity by discussing its purpose, sources of supply and demand, and problems. It was found that international liquidity serves primarily as a method of financing payments imbalances and maintaining stable exchange rates. The composition of liquidity has been affected by problems of confidence, for various reserve assets have proved to be of greater durability and stability in value than others. A breakdown of market or asset convertibility can lead to an intensification of Gresham's Law, in which the bad, overvalued money drives the undervalued money out of circulation. The need for liquidity, suggesting objective and subjective dimensions, implies that only qualitative assessments of reserve adequacy and optimality can be made, since quantitative indicators are limited by the nature of their sole use of objective variables.

CHAPTER 4

The Gold Standard in Theory and Practice

INTRODUCTION

During the seventeenth and eighteenth centuries, gold coins were considered the primary source of national currencies. The gold standard was officially recognized in 1816, when Britain adopted the gold sovereign as the basis of its monetary system. With Britain gaining prominence as the world's financial center during the nineteenth century, gold emerged as the principal source of liquidity.

During its golden era of 1880–1914, the gold standard generally witnessed such a high ratio of gold reserves to the money supply that domestic money was essentially equivalent to foreign exchange. The maintenance of confidence in the gold value of currencies became a primary objective of monetary authorities, who made extensive use of internal adjustments to cope with destabilizing external forces. In Diagram 2-5, the gold standard's operation is best represented by point D, which suggests almost complete reliance upon domestic deflation and inflation to reduce payments disequilibrium. The purpose of this chapter is to investigate the theoretical and empirical implications of the gold standard; of particular importance is the degree to which the gold standard in theory corresponded to its actual operation during the late nineteenth and early twentieth centuries.

Theory of the Gold Standard

Gold Standard Conditions and Variations. The theoretical model of the gold standard is structured upon assumptions of classical economic theory: a fully employed economy in the long run; a market system based on pure competition and a laissez faire role for government; upward and downward flexibility of prices and wages; money's sole function being a medium of exchange; and slowly changing institutions which affect money's transaction role. The classical writers largely contended that external and internal balance could be maintained in the long run if governments adhered to a common international monetary standard and certain rules of conduct.[1]

There are several essential rules that must be observed by all monetary authorities who operate under a gold standard. First, the national monetary authority must take steps to stipulate the official gold value of its currency, known as the mint price. This could be achieved in two equivalent ways: define the gold content of each currency unit, or define the currency price of each unit of gold. For example, prior to 1933, when the U.S. was on the gold standard, the dollar was defined as containing 23.22 grains of fine gold, implying a price of $20.67 per ounce (one troy ounce of gold is 480 grains). Second, at the mint price all the metal that is offered to the monetary authority will be purchased and coined; since one would not sell gold at a lower price for nonmonetary uses when the monetary authority agrees to purchase it at the mint price, the market price cannot fall below the official level. Third, to prevent the market price from rising above the mint price, the monetary authority must be willing to permit the melting of full-bodied gold coins (i.e., money that has just as much worth as a commodity as it has as money), thus fulfilling rising market demands for nonmonetary uses. Fourth, free movement of gold both at home and abroad must be maintained. Fifth, to ensure internal balance, there must be price and wage flexibility. Adhering to the above conditions implies that the value of gold is stabilized within narrow limits in terms of the domestic currency.

Price of Gold
(per Ounce)

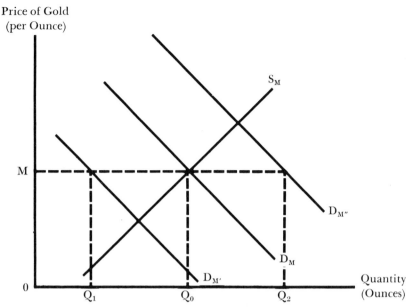

Diagram 4-1: Official Stabilization of the Price of Gold

Diagram 4-1 shows how the market price of gold cannot deviate from its mint price. Curve S_M represents the market supply of gold, while curve D_M denotes the market gold demand for non-monetary uses. The mint price is assumed to be OM. Suppose the market demand falls from D_M to $D_{M'}$. At the official price the market supplies Q_0-Q_1 excess quantities of gold. To prevent gold's price from falling below OM, the monetary authority purchases all gold offered by the market at that price; in effect, the market demand is increased by quantity Q_0-Q_1. Now suppose that the market demand rises from D_M to $D_{M''}$, signifying excess quantities demanded at the mint price. To maintain that price, the monetary authority allows full-bodied gold coins to be melted in sufficient quantities to augment the market supply by quantity Q_0-Q_2.

The above analysis suggests that the official supply and demand curves of gold for monetary uses are perfectly elastic at the mint price, at which the market price is stabilized. This is shown in Diagram 4-2, where curves S_M and D_M represent the market gold supply and demand for nonmonetary uses respectively, while curves S_0 and D_0 respectively signify the official supply of gold from melting full-bodied gold coins and the official gold demand for monetary purposes.[2] A major implication of the gold standard is that the maintenance of the mint price above the market level results in the monetary authorities losing control of the quantity of full-bodied coins, since the amount of gold available for monetary purposes is the residual of the total gold stock minus the quantities needed for nonmonetary purposes which is generally beyond control of monetary authorities. In Diagram 4-2, the official value of monetary gold equals area PQRS; this is found by subtracting from the market quantity supplied (OS) the quantity absorbed by nonmonetary purposes (OP), and multiplying that by the mint price (OM).

Under the gold specie standard, commonly known as the gold coin standard, all legal tender money consists of full-bodied gold coins. Since gold bullion can be converted into coin at the mint, and because gold coin can legally be melted down by anyone into gold bullion, the value of gold coin equals that of gold for other purposes. The value of currency always equals that of a given weight of gold, excluding the cost of minting, due to the full convertibility between gold and all forms of currency. Under the

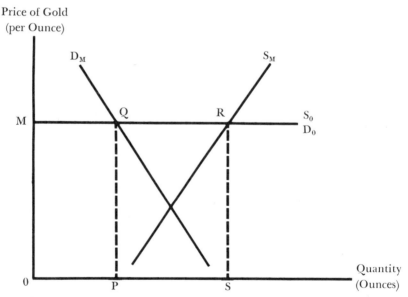

Diagram 4-2: Relation of Monetary and Nonmonetary Gold Supply and Demand

gold specie standard, a 100 percent reserve principle exists, for gold reserves are always equal to the domestic supply of money.

Under the gold bullion standard gold coins are not minted, and convertibility is restricted to transactions in bullion. Because gold coins no longer serve as a form of legal tender and a medium of exchange in common transactions, they tend to be withdrawn from circulation, converted into gold bars, and used in large transactions, particularly in international trade. The gold bullion standard can also fulfill the 100 percent reserve principle; if the monetary authorities permit banks to freely buy and sell gold against notes or bank deposits, and keep them completely covered with gold, there is full equality between the total amount of gold reserves and the domestic money supply. Historically, the rise of demand deposits in the major gold standard countries during the late 1800s and early 1900s led to a fractional reserve principle, whereby a given amount of gold reserves could support a larger amount of domestic money.

Under the gold exchange standard, gold coins are not put into circulation, nor is there convertibility of domestic currency into gold. Its purpose is to economize on gold. One country can operate a gold exchange standard without increasing the demand for gold if it holds the notes or liabilities of a country which agrees to convert its currency obligations into gold bullion upon request of foreign holders. The gold exchange standard is a practical recognition of the use of paper currency as a domestic and international medium of exchange.

Exchange Rate Stabilization: Gold Points. For countries on the gold standard, stable exchange rates were maintained via private arbitragers, who made a riskless profit by taking advantage of exchange rate differentials existing between points of time or geographic locations. How this operates is illustrated by the case of the U.S. and Britain prior to the 1930s, when they were on the gold standard.

At that time, one dollar was worth 23.22 grains of gold, while the pound contained approximately 113 grains of gold. Since there was a fixed quantity of gold in the national monetary units, a par rate of exchange could be determined by comparing their gold contents. Because the pound contained approximately 4.86 times as much gold as the dollar (i.e., $113/23.22 = 4.8665$), the par rate equaled approximately \$4.86. Induced by imbalances in the foreign exchange market, the market rate could deviate from the official rate. However, actual market fluctuation was limited by the cost of transporting gold, which included not only the weighing, insuring, and carting costs of shipping gold abroad but also the loss of interest while the metal was being transported and the profits of bankers who handled the transaction. Any exchange rate fluctuation greater than the amount attributed to transportation costs would induce gold or capital flows.

Assume that the official exchange rate is $4.86 per pound, that the U.S. fixes the price of gold at $4.86 per 0.235 ounce while Britain fixes gold's price at £1 for 0.235 ounce (during the early 1900s the pound contained 113 grains of gold and one ounce equaled 480 grains; one pound equaled $113/480 = 0.235$ ounce of gold). Also assume that the cost of shipping each 0.235 ounce across the Atlantic is $0.02. The market rate could freely fluctuate within a range of $4.84 and $4.88 before private arbitragers would find it profitable to take advantage of the exchange rate differentials between the two countries. This is illustrated in Diagrams 4-3 and 4-4.

In Diagram 4-3, representing the New York market for British pounds, curve S_0 denotes the New York supply of pounds, while curve D_0 denotes the New York demand for pounds. Sup-

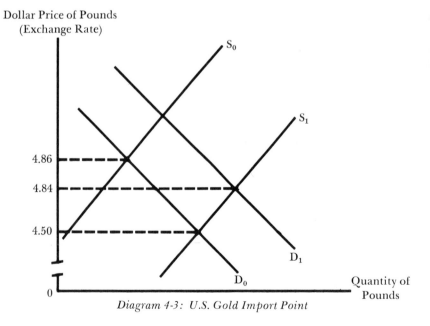

Dollar Price of Pounds
(Exchange Rate)

Diagram 4-3: U.S. Gold Import Point

pose a U.S. trade surplus with Britain increases the supply of pounds from S_0 to S_1, thus reducing the market rate from \$4.86 to \$4.50. A reduction in the market exchange rate implies the dollar's appreciation relative to the pound, because each pound now buys only 4.5 dollars rather than 4.86 dollars. An increase in the market exchange rate suggests the dollar's depreciation relative to the pound, since each pound now buys more dollars. It would pay an arbitrager to exchange \$4.50 for £1 on the foreign exchange market, use that pound to purchase 0.235 ounce of gold from Britain's central bank, ship it to the U.S., and sell it to the U.S. Treasury for \$4.86. A profit of \$0.34 would be made (i.e., \$0.36 minus the \$0.02 transportation cost). As long as the market rate was below \$4.84 this practice would continue, ultimately forcing the market rate towards the official level, since the arbitragers' demand for pounds would be increasing from D_0 towards D_1. Therefore, gold flows from Britain to the U.S. prevent the market rate from falling below \$4.84; this limit is called the U.S. gold import point.

Diagram 4-4 suggests how the upper limit on the market rate cannot exceed \$4.88. Suppose a British trade surplus with the U.S. results in an increase in the U.S. demand for pounds from

Dollar Price of Pounds
(Exchange Rate)

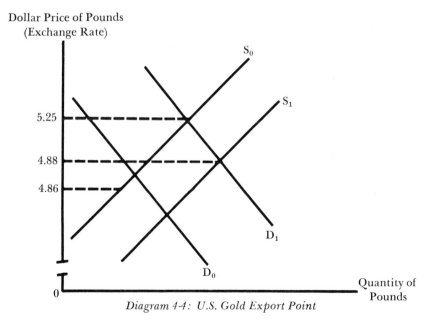

Diagram 4-4: U.S. Gold Export Point

D_0 to D_1, which initially increases the market rate to $5.25. It would now pay a British arbitrager to convert £1 into $5.25 on the foreign exchange market, use that $5.25 to purchase 0.254 ounce of gold from the U.S. Treasury (i.e., $5.25/4.86 \times 0.235 = 0.254$), ship it to Britain, and sell it to the Bank of England for 1.08 pounds. He would make slightly less than 0.08 pound profit, since the $0.02 shipping costs must be subtracted. As long as the market rate was above $4.88 this practice would continue, which ultimately increases the supply of pounds from S_0 towards S_1 and forces the market rate back towards the official level. Therefore, the gold outflows from the U.S. prevent the market rate from rising above $4.88; this limit is called the U.S. gold export point.

The above analysis suggests that, within the gold points, the market rate can freely fluctuate according to international supply-and-demand forces. However, once the gold points are reached, the supply-and-demand curves of foreign exchange become perfectly elastic, providing a boundary beyond which the market rate cannot deviate.

Diagram 4-5 shows how the foreign demand for gold can be satisfied by gold exports. Assuming perfectly elastic demand and supply curves of foreign exchange at the gold points, suppose the

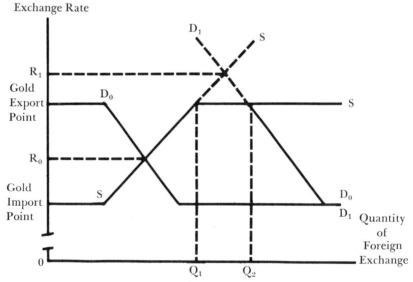

Diagram 4-5: Gold Exports Fulfilling the Demand for Foreign Exchange

demand rises from D_0 to D_1, initially pushing the market rate from R_0 to R_1. Because foreign arbitragers now find it profitable to convert foreign currency into domestic gold, gold exports must equal Q_1-Q_2 per period to maintain the gold export point. Similarly, suppose the supply of foreign exchange increases from S_0 to S_1 in Diagram 4-6, initially forcing the exchange rate below the gold import point, to R_1. To satisfy domestic arbitragers, gold imports must equal Q_1-Q_2 to maintain the gold import point.[3]

Exchange Rate

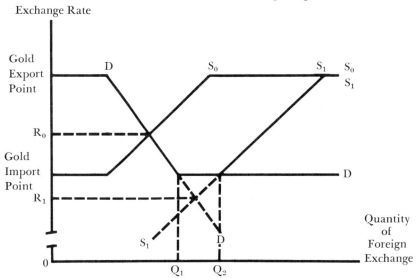

Diagram 4-6: Gold Imports Fulfilling the Supply of Foreign Exchange

Several implications can be drawn from the above analysis. First, if the supply-and-demand curves of foreign exchange intersect within the gold points, there are no profit-motivated international gold movements, for private arbitragers cannot profit from exchange rate differentials between nations. Second, if the supply-and-demand curves of foreign exchange initially intersect outside the gold points, the actions of private arbitragers tend to force the market rate back towards the official rate. Thus the upper and lower limits on exchange rate movements are determined by the cost of transporting gold from one financial center to another. Third, although gold movements are signs of imbalances in the foreign exchange market, short-term capital flows may also indicate disequilibriums. Suppose a rise in the market rate toward the gold export point is associated with expectations that it is temporary. This may induce foreign dealers to acquire the temporarily cheap domestic currency, the result being an increase in the supply of foreign exchange which restrains the increase in the market rate. In the opposite case of a fall in the market rate towards the gold import point, domestic dealers may acquire the temporarily cheap foreign currency. These capital outflows would restrain the decline in the market rate, thus being a partial substitute for gold movements.[4]

Gold Standard Adjustment: Price-Specie-Flow Mechanism. Because the gold standard was committed to narrow exchange rate movements within the gold points, the maintenance of an economy's overall balance required internal rather than external adjustments. Also, the philosophy of the gold standard was based on a laissez-faire role for government and a free market system, hence excluding discretionary expenditure-switching or -changing policies. A major indication of external disequilibrium was international gold or short-term capital movements, due to disequilibriums in the foreign exchange market. Based on a price-specie-flow mechanism, classical economic theory envisioned an automatic adjustment mechanism in which external balance could be attained primarily through price effects induced by international gold movements.[5]

Under the traditional theory, a country with a deficit payments position loses gold, while a surplus country gains gold. According to the quantity theory of money, the price level varies directly with the money supply in circulation. This theory is based upon the equation of exchange, one common form being $MV = PQ$. Here M is the quantity of money, V its velocity, P the general price level, and Q the level of output. In the deficit country, a lower M induces a proportionate drop in P since it is assumed that Q is at full employment and V constant in the short run; thus changes in monetary variables induce no change in the real variables. The surplus country, facing gold inflows and monetary expansion, finds its prices rising. Depending on the price elasticities of demand, this causes the deficit country to substitute domestically produced goods for imports in its purchases, while the opposite occurs in the surplus country. Therefore, the balance of trade normally moves in favor of the deficit country and against the surplus country, and automatically reduces the external disequilibrium. The price-specie-flow mechanism consists of three main stages: a link between the balance of payments and the money supply; the link between the money supply and the price level; the link between the price level and the balance of payments.[6]

Although not largely emphasized until the advent of Keynesian macroeconomic theory, there are two other automatic adjustment effects of the gold standard—the interest rate and income effects. Because these effects are interdependent, they will be discussed together.

Under the interest rate effect, changes in relative interest rates due to international gold movements may induce equilibrating capital flows. Suppose that due to capital movements from country X to country Y the former has a deficit payments position while the latter has a surplus. Country X therefore exports gold, which decreases its money supply and induces rising interest rates. At the same time, country Y faces gold inflows, and consequently rising money supplies, which induce falling interest rates. This discourages foreign investments by X while Y is encouraged to invest abroad. The result is an automatic net capital flow from Y to X that reduced the former's surplus and the latter's deficit.

In the above example, interest rates were assumed to induce international capital movements. However, investment is also a function of the rate of interest. And changes in investment affect national income through the multiplier, which induces changes in imports by the extent of the marginal propensity to import. For a deficit country, the initial gold outflow automatically reduces the domestic money supply, which promotes an increase in interest rates; this induces falling levels of investment spending that, via the multiplier, reduce the level of national income. At the same time, the opposite forces operate in the surplus country. As a result, the deficit country's imports decline while those of the surplus country increase; the external disequilibriums are automatically reduced. The success of the income effect depends upon the marginal propensities to save and import and the interest elasticity of the investment demand and the demand for money.[7]

The essence of the gold standard adjustment mechanism is that countries must be willing to permit internal adjustments to attain overall balance. This ideally required central bankers to obey the "rules of the game." Not only was there to be an absence of offsetting policies to counteract external disequilibriums, but central banks must actively reinforce and speed up the adjustment process by either lowering the discount rate and buying securities on the open market for a gold-gaining country, or raising the discount rate and selling securities on the open market for a country losing gold.

Diagram 4-7 illustrates an alternative view of the gold standard adjustment process. Curve FF represents the combination of income and interest rate levels that provide external balance. It is positively sloped since there is a direct relation between a payment surplus and the interest rate, while an inverse relation exists between a payment surplus and the income level. To illustrate, assume that point Q represents a combination of interest rates and income levels at which there is external balance. Now sup-

Interest Rate

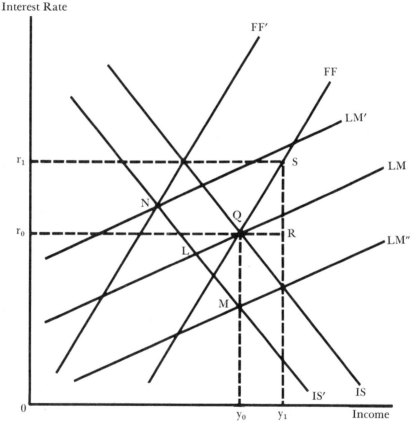

Diagram 4-7: Restoration of General Equilibrium for a Deficit Country
under the Gold Standard

pose that income increases from y_0 to y_1 while the interest rate remains constant at r_0. As the higher income level induces rising imports, an external deficit appears. To regain external balance, the interest rate must rise to some level greater than r_0, say r_1, to induce capital inflows or reduce capital outflows in sufficient amounts to offset the payment deficit. Thus, the FF curve is positively sloped.

After adjustments have occurred, any combination of interest rates and income levels that signify a point to the right of FF denotes a payments deficit, while one to the left represents a surplus. Shifts in FF are caused by external balance disequilibriums. Starting from equilibrium point E, due to an exogenous decrease in world demand suppose country A experiences a deficit payments position. If A wishes to maintain its original income level, y_0, it must permit an increase in the interest rate, therefore shifting curve FF to FF'. Similarly, suppose that due to increasing foreign interest rates, A faces capital outflows which result in a deficit payments position. Because A must allow falling income levels in order to maintain the initial interest rate, r_0, curve FF shifts to FF'. Thus, a payments deficit results in a leftward shift, while a payments surplus denotes the opposite. Curve IS represents combinations of income and interest rates at which investment equals saving; it is negatively sloped because a fall in the interest rate induces higher investment spending which, through the multiplier, results in a higher income level. Equilibrium in the money market is illustrated by the positively sloped LM curve; since rising income levels imply a larger portion of the money supply to be used for transactionary purposes, there is a smaller share for idle balances, hence pushing up the rate of interest.

Starting at the position of overall balance, point Q, suppose that due to foreign competition a fall in country A's exports results in a deficit payments position. Three ensuing effects imply the movement towards short-run equilibrium at point N. The opposite forces would symmetrically occur in a surplus country, thus reinforcing the equilibrating adjustment effects. This symmetrical adjustment mechanism was a distinct feature of the theoretical gold standard. Chapter 5 points out that a major limitation of the dollar-gold system was its asymmetrical adjustment mechanism in which the deficit countries were forced to bear the greatest adjustment burdens. First, due to the deficit FF shifts leftward. Second, because a reduction in exports induces a fall in domestic spending, income will contract according to the size of the foreign trade multiplier (i.e., change in income = change in exports × 1/marginal propensity to save + marginal propensity to import); the IS curve thus shifts leftward toward IS'. Third, because the money supply is directly tied to the balance of payments, the gold outflow implies that LM shifts leftward to LM'. The eventual restoration of overall equilibrium at point Q requires the deficit country to undergo internal adjustments in the forms of higher interest rates and falling income and price levels. Since these adjustments do not necessarily guarantee the immediate attainment of full equilibrium, it is necessary to point out the essential conditions for full adjustment.[8]

With regard to achieving full adjustment, a first point is that there generally must be a major change in the level of economic activity. Classical economic theory, relying primarily on flexible price and wage adjustments, never emphasized this stage; only if prices and wages are extremely flexible will the need for income adjustments be reduced. Second, even if the "rules of the game" are not obeyed and central banks are totally passive, full adjustment may occur solely due to changes in the levels of economic activity and prices in the deficit and surplus countries. A third point is that adjustment will not likely be successful if there are perverse price expectations in which price changes suggest exaggerated expectations of continued price changes. The last point is that if the sum of the price elasticities of demand for a country's exports and imports is sufficiently small, shifts in demand between deficit and surplus countries may suggest less money being spent on the goods that are becoming cheaper, and more money being spent on the goods becoming more expensive. To illustrate this point, we assume a two-country model in which country A's import demand elasticity equals 0.2 while country B's equals zero. Due to a trade deficit, suppose gold outflows induce monetary contraction sufficient to result in a 10 percent price decline in A, while a trade surplus induces a 10 percent price rise in B. Country A would find the value of its imports rising, for the 10 percent price increase in B would induce only a 2 percent decline in the quantity of A's imports. In terms of A's currency, the value of A's exports would fall since the 10 percent price decline in A would not induce any changes in B's import demand.

Classical theory contended that external and internal balance would be maintained for countries on the gold standard. Even if this conclusion is true, the adjustment period may be very long, involving costly recessions and inflations. From the previous discussion it is apparent that a rapid adjustment requires the fulfillment of several factors.[9] Strict obedience to the "rules of the game" by central bankers suggests the use of discount rate policy to influence the rate of interest which affects domestic spending and capital flows. It is also desirable that there is wage and price flexibility in both directions, so that relatively minor changes in economic activity induce large price movements. In addition, the sum of the demand elasticities should be high, perhaps four, five, or six, for substantial adjustment to take place through internal price changes.[10] Finally, perverse speculative effects must be minimized in that price movements must not lead to exaggerated expectations of continued price changes.

Although the classical theory of the gold standard provided a long-run adjustment mechanism, it was not without limitations. The greatest difficulty in practicing the adjustment mechanism involved the subordination of domestic policies to external balance priorities. Because exchange rate variations were limited to small movements around the gold points, correcting an external disequilibrium required internal adjustments in prices, incomes, and employment. As will be later discussed, countries that are committed to full employment and price stability as economic goals may not accept costly internal adjustments. Instead, by using the reserve requirement, discount rate, or open market operations, central banks may divorce their money supplies from the balance of payments. Whatever neutralization method is used, the result is to counteract the adjustment mechanism.

Diagram 4-7 suggests that as a result of an external deficit, the automatic adjustment mechanism initially carried the equilibrium to point N, whereby, in the long run the process would reverse itself and reestablish overall balance at point Q. Suppose deficit country A refuses to accept the "rules of the game" and uses open market purchases and lower discount rates to neutralize the gold outflow and keep curve LM in its original position. A new partial equilibrium would be established at point L, in which there is equilibrium in the goods and money markets but an external deficit. However, if a full employment income level is the primary national objective, by increasing the money supply to the point where LM shifts to LM″, national income can be stabilized at the original income level. Because supplies of reserves and the ability of monetary authorities to maintain the stock of money tend to be limited, neutralization policies unaccompanied by internal or external adjustments are restricted to the short run.[11]

Another disadvantage of the theoretical gold standard is that if gold's value does not remain stable, the effects are directly transmitted into the value of money. The general price level may partly depend upon gold mining costs as well as the nonmonetary demand for gold.

THE GOLD STANDARD IN PRACTICE

The years 1880–1914 are usually described in economic textbooks as the golden age of the gold standard, for the conditions prior to World War I often approximated the previously mentioned theoretical factors. Although the late nineteenth century succeeded in preserving free trade and exchange rate stability for a large part of the world, most of the benefits may have been passed on to the industrially advanced countries which formed the core of the system.[12] Nevertheless, several stabilizing elements were present that effectively combated violent cyclical fluctuations in world economic activity.

A primary reason why economic disturbances did not seriously upset external balance in the world prior to 1914 was that long-term capital movements of the core countries, particularly Britain, were appropriate to the industrial structures of both lending and borrowing countries. Because there was a tendency for British balance of trade and long-term capital flows to be inversely related in cyclical fluctuations, there was a basic stabilizing influence. Also, government controls and tariffs were not employed to correct temporary external imbalances during periods of depression; consequently, the price mechanism was largely left free to exert a stabilizing influence. Furthermore, problems of confidence in the payments mechanism and political system were rare; thus there was an absence of technical strains which questioned the prominence of London as the world's financial center. And last, although the "rules of the game" were not universally obeyed, interest rates and capital flows often moved in the right direction without active central bank support.[13]

Price and Wage Adjustments. According to the nineteenth-century gold standard, it was essential for the supply of international reserves, notably gold, to increase at a rate adequate to finance growing world production and transactions, as well as to ensure sufficient reserves needed for exchange convertibility and stability. During the 1872–1896 period, the rate of world output growth relative to that of world gold production was sufficient to create downward pressures on prices; during that era wholesale prices fell 50 percent in the U.S., while falling 39 percent, 36 percent, and 43 percent in Britain, Germany, and France, respectively.[14] It was not until the discovery of new gold mines in the U.S. and South Africa, and of new processes for working old gold mines during the 1890s that the liquidity shortage was eased. The annual rate of world gold production increased from 5.1 million ounces during 1881–1890, to 10.2 million in 1891–1900, and to 18.3 million in 1901–1910.[15] The world inflationary era of 1896–1913 is generally attributed to the increased supplies of money coming mainly from expanded world gold production; during that period U.S. price levels rose 49 percent, while those of Britain, Germany, and France rose 32 percent, 41 percent, and 41 percent respectively.[16]

According to the quantity theory of money, countries experiencing gold inflows would face rising price levels while deficit countries would experience falling price levels. However, it has been suggested that there was a large degree of parallel price movements between deficit and surplus countries. One study questions the equilibrating role of the price mechanism by showing that despite wide variations in export values, measured in current dollars for the eleven leading trading nations of the world in the 1870–1960 period, prices moved in the same direction in 89 percent of the observed movements.[17] It also has been shown that among the countries which maintained stable exchange rates under the gold standard, downward wage adjustments generally were of minor consequence. Whenever excessive inflations were allowed to develop, external balance was generally restored through devaluations rather than internal adjustments.[18]

Monetary Policy. Prior to World War I, the major objective of monetary policy in the gold standard countries was to maintain the convertibility of the national currency into gold at the official exchange rate. This would provide a system of fixed exchange rates, since movements within the gold points were negligible. Although economic textbooks often assume that the classical adjustment mechanism was automatic in that monetary policy mechanically responded to gold flows, governments did in fact resort to discretionary policies to maintain convertibility.[19] For instance, the manipulation of the gold points was sometimes used to affect the short-term capital and/or gold flows between countries. During the 1890s the central banks of France and England would at certain times raise their selling prices for gold bars, which was equivalent to raising the gold export point. This was intended to widen the margin of exchange rate flexibility around parity, thus reducing the necessity of raising interest rates to attract short-term capital flows. Another discretionary policy on the part of central bankers was the intervention in the foreign exchange market to prevent excessive movements of the exchange rate, particularly toward the gold export point, at which private arbitragers would profit from exchange rate differentials. These policies were chiefly carried out by the Austro-Hungarian Bank.[20] The above examples do not imply that the stabilization of economic activity was a primary objective of monetary policy, but they do suggest that the so-called automatic adjustment mechanism was really not so automatic.

In the pre-1914 era, the primary technique of monetary policy was discount policy which regulated the cost of central bank credit to member banks; a rise in the discount rate would make credit more expensive, thus discouraging an expansion in the money supply, while a lowering of the discount rate implied the opposite. According to the "rules of the game," central bankers were to actively promote adjustments in the internal and external balance by lowering the discount rate in the surplus countries, to induce fewer short-term capital imports and/or greater capital exports; the opposite policy applied for deficit countries. However, central bankers often disrupted the adjustment mechanism's operation through neutralization policies which divorced the money supply from the balance of payments; rather than supporting monetary contraction in deficit countries and expansion in surplus countries, central bankers neutralized the gold flows through offsetting discount policies. One study found that rather than being the exception, neutralization policies were adopted. This suggests that the "rules of the game" were badly obeyed before 1914, as they were thereafter.[21]

Private Short-Term Capital Movements. It is generally accepted that short-term capital flows were an important aspect of a successfully operating gold standard.[22] Besides financing international transactions, these movements, sensitive to changes of exchange rates within the gold points and interest rate differentials, played an equilibrating role by reducing the need for official reserves in times of external imbalance. A fall in the exchange rate to the gold import point tended to induce capital outflows, since domestic dealers would buy the temporarily cheap foreign exchange. Conversely, when the exchange rate rose to the gold export point, foreign dealers would find it profitable to buy the temporarily cheap domestic currency, thus inducing capital inflows. It was felt that these capital flows would be equilibrating in that they counteract exchange rate movements out of the gold points.

However, one study suggests that the pre-1914 gold standard witnessed "hot money" movements caused by disequilibrating capital flows and exchange speculation. First, capital movements were not always equilibrating in character, because not all types of capital flows were induced by the rate of interest or exchange rates.[23] Second, such funds were not always perfectly mobile internationally; this may account in part for the relatively large short-term interest rate differentials among the leading gold standard countries in the pre-1914 years.[24] Third, although "hot money" movements did not reach the proportions compared to the post World War I era, they were of major consequence. These abnormal capital movements, associated with destabilizing speculation and the desire to avoid capital losses due to exogenous factors, such as anticipated wars, political crises, etc., often perversely flowed from deficit to surplus countries and from high to low interest rate countries. For instance, in 1905–1906 Russia came under speculative attack due to fears that she would abandon gold convertibility following the Russo-Japanese War of 1904–1905. For countries not members of the gold standard group prior to 1914 (i.e., Spain, Greece, and many of the Latin American countries), destabilizing speculation may have accentuated the degree of exchange rate fluctuations.[25]

Role of Key Currencies. As discussed earlier, a key currency must fulfill several functions; official and private foreigners must willingly hold it for a significant duration of time and in sizable quantities; also, it must serve as a vehicle currency by having the capacity to finance international transactions. Although gold movements may have been used for official settlements under the gold standard, during the 1900–1914 period most private international settlements were conducted by key currencies, notably British pounds, French francs, and German marks. These countries performed the role of a world banker on a scale unmatched before or since. Unlike today, when key currencies derive their significance from serving as medias of international settlement and reserves, the emergence of key currencies during the nineteenth century gained prestige from the full asset convertibility of paper money into gold.[26]

Although the largest proportion of the growth of official monetary reserves in absolute terms between 1880 and 1913 was provided by gold, in percentage terms key currencies began to grow relative to gold reserves during the 1900–1913 period. During this time, foreign exchange accumulations grew 10.8 percent annually, well above the 6.3 percent annual rate of gold reserve growth. Both of these growth rates surpassed those of world manufacturing output and the value of world trade, which were 3.9 and 5.3 percent respectively.[27] These imply that the pre-1914 gold standard witnessed the introduction of key currencies as reserve assets, which would become officially recognized during the gold exchange standard era.

The Post-1914 Gold Standard. By disrupting the flow of trade and investments in Europe, World War I dealt the gold standard a blow from which it never recovered. During the war all major countries abandoned not only the gold standard, but all fiscal and monetary discipline as well. The result was high inflation; by the early 1920s, the price level expressed in national currencies at their pre-war parities had risen 60 to 100 percent. However, because the price of gold remained constant while the costs of gold mining increased, the production of new gold fell, hence inducing fear of a liquidity crisis.[28]

The 1922 Genoa Economic Agreement recommended the formal adoption of a gold exchange standard in order to economize on gold; under this standard, international reserves consist of both gold and reserve currencies. While official implementation of the agreements never took place, most countries allowed their central bankers to use as reserves those key currencies that were backed by gold. Of the twenty-five major countries' total reserves, foreign exchange ranged 19–27 percent from 1924–1926, and as high as 42 percent in 1927–1928.[29] From the viewpoint that gold could be economized, the gold exchange standard was quite successful prior to 1930.

The return to gold during the 1920s never worked out as satisfactorily as the pre-war gold standard. One explanation is that the gold exchange standard further weakened the classical adjustment mechanism. This was because during the 1920s central bankers generally refused to adhere to the "rules of the game" and to actively use monetary policy to reinforce equilibrating adjustments. Instead, central bankers of deficit countries often attempted to neutralize the contractionary effects upon internal balance through expansionary policies. The direct link between external disequilibriums and the money supply was severed. Other post-World War I strains included a lack of confidence in the political and economic systems in Europe, increasing internal rigidities which reduced the flexibility of prices, and the choice of inappropriate gold parities following World War I, notably by Britain. With the Great Depression, financial chaos spread throughout Europe. The resulting loss of confidence in the pound caused central bankers to make runs on Britain's gold; in 1931 Britain was forced to abandon the gold standard. By 1932 the crisis had spread to the U.S. Withdrawals of gold from the country led President Roosevelt to terminate the gold standard for the U.S. in 1933.

The ideal theory of the gold standard provided several advantages. First, a laissez-faire role for government coincided with the prevailing notions of individualism and liberty during the nineteenth century. Second, the free market system theoretically would provide an optimal allocation of resources in the long run. Third, the expectations of stable long-run prices would encourage international trade, finance, and investments. Although the pre–World War I gold standard was generally an era of economic and political harmony, especially for the major industrial nations, the above objectives were rarely, if ever, fully attained. Not only were the "rules of the game" often disobeyed, but there also occurred destabilizing speculation, attacks on weak currencies, etc., which disrupted the tranquility of the system. The post–World War I gold standard was never to regain its original prominence, for political and economic factors were no longer conducive to the ideal free market system which the gold standard required.

CHAPTER 5

The Dollar-Gold System

INTRODUCTION

A successfully functioning international payments mechanism must be assessed by its contribution to the basic global economic objectives. Among these are full employment, an adequate rate of economic growth, reasonably stable prices, and mutually beneficial trade that enhances an efficient international allocation of resources through freedom of international transactions.

In attempting to fulfill these goals, it is likely that some countries will from time to time develop external surpluses or deficits in varying magnitude and duration under a system of fixed exchange rates. If monetary reserves available to finance the imbalances are too large, deficit countries may make excessive claims and even impose inflationary pressures on their trading partners, instead of undergoing adjustments to restore external balance. Likewise, if reserves are inadequate to finance the deficits, countries may have to utilize monetary and fiscal expenditure-changing policies that depress the level of domestic economic activity to attain external equilibrium. There also may be occasional exogenous economic and political shocks which disrupt the payments mechanism. Unless it can adjust promptly and smoothly to such disturbances, the ensuing instability in the foreign exchange market may hinder an efficient pattern of trade, finance, and investments.[1]

In pursuing the above objectives, an international payments mechanism must function under several constraints. First, no individual country's external deficits or surpluses should be excessively large or prolonged. Second, correction of such imbalances should be achieved in ways that do not impose on individual countries, or the world as a whole, unacceptable inflation or deflation or physical restrictions on trade and payments. Third, a maximum sustainable growth of international transactions should be facilitated. Although there are differences of opinion on what constitutes "unacceptable" and "excessively large/prolonged," the success of an international payments system depends upon the extent to which it reasonably passes these tests in the eyes of most countries.

With the breakdown of international trade and finance during the 1930s, the international payments mechanism did not adequately fulfill the above objectives and tests. The 1944 international monetary agreement reached at Bretton Woods, New Hampshire, which called for the formation of the International Monetary Fund, was an attempt to restore an efficient payments system. Two proposals were considered for the basis of a new international monetary system—the American plan, authored by Harry White, and the British plan, authored by John Maynard Keynes. The White Plan won general approval of the participating nations, thus becoming the basis of the IMF. This chapter will analyze the nature and problem of the international monetary system, called the dollar-gold system, which lasted from the late 1940s until August 15, 1971.

ADJUSTABLE PEGGED EXCHANGE RATES

The creators of the IMF were well aware of the tragic monetary experience of the 1930s. With the collapse of the gold standard during the early 1930s due to the economic disturbances induced by the Great Depression, the world witnessed destabilizing fluctuating exchange rates caused by "hot money" movements and speculative capital flights, fear of competitive exchange rate depreciations, and the employment of exchange controls.

Since none of the above policies satisfactorily fulfilled global internal and external objectives, the Fund system was an attempt to combine some of the virtues of the gold standard with those of the system existing in the 1930s, while avoiding the disadvantages of both. The main obstacles to be avoided were the following: rigid exchange rates; the destabilizing influence of freely floating exchange rates; the gold standard's deflationary adjustment bias; the inefficient distortions caused by exchange controls; competitive exchange rate depreciations and conflicting national policies. The benefits hoped to be retained included the gold standard's stability, the adjustment efficiency of adjustable exchange rates, the selective use of exchange controls over exchange rates fluctuations.[2]

The Fund therefore adopted an adjustable peg system. Exchange rates were to be kept stable in the short run; however, in case of a "fundamental disequilibrium," the par rates could be changed via expenditure-switching devaluations or revaluations. Although never explicitly defined, a "fundamental disequilibrium" seemed to indicate a long-run persistent external imbalance, notably a deficit, which appeared unlikely to be reversed by monetary and fiscal expenditure-changing policies. The IMF chose not to define this term in order to prevent speculators from making sizable profits from exchange rate movements. But these limits were restricted; a nation could automatically change its currency's par value up to 10 percent—any change greater than this required permission of the Fund. However, in practice this rule was not strictly followed.

Gold Exchange Standard

Although traces of the gold exchange standard appeared during the late 1800s and early 1900s, it was not until the 1922 Genoa Economic Agreement that the need for a gold exchange standard became officially recognized. This practice of including reserve currencies as reserve assets in order to economize on gold was informally adopted during the 1920s. It required that the reserve centers maintain asset convertibility by being willing to convert their currency liabilities into gold upon request of foreign holders. There were two major motives for maintaining asset convertibility; first, reserve centers believed that as the world's banker, their international prestige was enhanced; second, reserve currencies could be held in a form which earned interest income, while gold holdings provided a zero yield. The Great Depression resulted in a termination of the gold exchange standard. By increasing the price of gold during the 1930s, competitive devaluations temporarily provided gold with a positive return in the form of a capital gain, which exceeded the return on reserve currency holdings. Also, both short- and long-run confidence problems existed, for frequent devaluations made questionable the stability of currencies' values. Therefore, many countries abandoned the gold exchange standard by changing the composition of their reserves from currencies into gold.[3]

The reestablishment of the gold exchange standard following World War II involved no formal agreement. Diagram 5-1 suggests that during the late 1940s and early 1950s, the U.S. dollar and gold were the major components of global reserves, while Britain's role as a world banker declined.

The dollar fulfilled all of the essential conditions of an international currency: it was a medium of payment for settlements of private international transactions; it fulfilled the role of an intervention currency by being used to maintain the value of national currencies in the foreign exchange market; it was a store of value for holding international assets; it was a unit of account for measuring the value of international transactions.[4] Because global dollar holdings were more desirable than gold, due to their interest earnings and asset convertibility, U.S. payment deficits were welcome during the early 1950s as a source of reserves for the reconstructing European countries. Therefore, the U.S. assumed the role of a world banker largely because of its financial strength relative to other nations. The gold exchange standard, which existed until the monetary crisis of August, 1971, was the result of an informal agreement whereby the U.S. passively accepted the role of a reserve center and source of international liquidity. Although gold remained the de jure numeraire, in that all official par values at the IMF were defined in terms of gold, the dollar became the de facto international numeraire.

Economizing on Gold. The principal idea underlying the gold exchange standard was to economize on gold. This is discussed below.[5]

Assume a world of many nations that are initially on the gold standard; one of them is called the reserve center, while the others

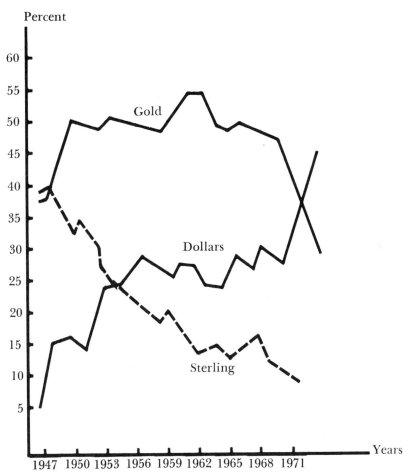

Diagram 5-1: Composition of International Reserves under the Gold Exchange Standard

together are called the ROW. Suppose they decide to adopt a gold exchange standard. The following conditions must be met. First, the ROW agrees to turn over all existing and newly mined gold at a fixed price to the reserve center, which in return issues its currency obligations, maintains full asset convertibility, pays interest to foreign holders of its currency, and agrees to hold only gold as reserves. Second, the ROW's central bankers agree to accept the currency obligations in settlements as equivalent to gold. Third, the reserve center can issue its currency obligations in excess of its gold assets, provided that it maintains a minimal acceptable reserve ratio (i.e., gold assets/currency obligations).

Suppose that the reserve center maintains a reserve ratio of 25 percent. Then $1,000 of gold supports $4,000 of currency obligations and $5,000 of total reserves. If the reserve ratio falls to 20 percent, the extent of gold economizing increases, for currency obligations could expand to $5,000 while total reserves grow to $6,000.

Based on the above assumptions, Diagram 5-2 represents a simplified model of a gold exchange standard. At time t_0 a 25 percent reserve ratio exists, denoted by the ratio OA/AB. Suppose that during the period t_0-t_1, gold increases by rate r, the slope of line G_0. Given the initial reserve ratio, currency obligations will expand by rate r', the slope of line C_0. Diagram 5-1 assumes that the slope (i.e., m) of G_0 is 1/8. Therefore, the maximum slope that C_0 can have to maintain the 25 percent reserve ratio as gold and currency obligations grow over time is 1/2. The growth of gold therefore determines the expansion of currency obligations and total reserves.

Now assume that during the period t_1-t_2 the rate of gold growth decreases to s, the slope of segment G_1. To maintain the initial 25 percent reserve ratio, currency obligations must expand by s' (i.e., s'<r'), the slope of segment C_1. Between time periods t_1-t_2, gold grows at rate s, the slope of G_1, whose value is assumed to be 1/10 (i.e., r > s). Therefore, the maximum slope of C_1 must be 2/5

$$\left(\text{i.e., } \frac{1/10}{1/m} = \frac{1/8}{1/2}; m = 2/5 \right).$$

If it is desirable to maintain the initial currency obligation growth rate r', given a lower gold growth rate s, the monetary authority must economize on gold by lowering the reserve ratio to 20 percent. This is shown at t_2 by the ratio CD/DG.

The conclusions of this model are twofold. First, if a given reserve ratio is maintained over time, the growth of currency obligations and total reserves is determined solely by the growth of gold. Second, if the rate of gold growth decreases, currency obligations and total reserves may continue to grow at their initial rate, provided that the reserve ratio decreases; gold is economized since a given stock supports a larger quantity of total reserves.

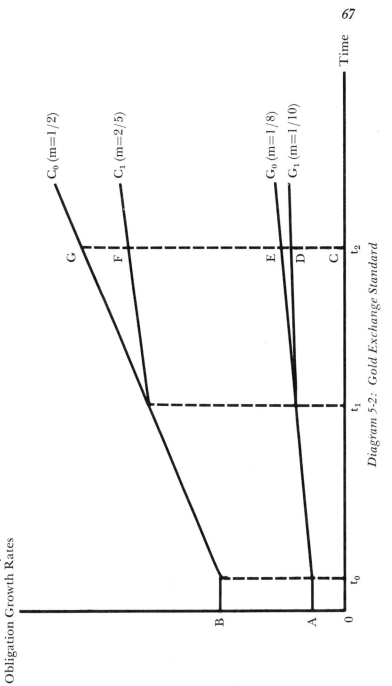

Diagram 5-2: Gold Exchange Standard

Exchange Rate Stabilization—Par and Cross Rates. For a successful gold exchange standard to exist, several conditions must be met. As mentioned earlier, the reserve center must maintain full asset convertibility; by allowing foreign holders of its currency obligations to convert them into gold, confidence in the value of the reserve currency is maintained. Because this suggests that under a multi-asset system, gold and reserve currencies must be viewed to be of equal quality and value, the reserve center's reserve ratio must not deteriorate over time. Therefore, the net growth rate of payments deficits by the reserve center must not exceed the growth of its gold assets over time. Under the gold exchange standard, the U.S. was the only country to maintain asset convertibility; the rest of the world maintained market convertibility, whereby any holder of a currency, say sterling, cannot use it only to buy and invest in Britain, but also to convert it into any other currency at the existing exchange rate.

A second condition is that each central bank defines and supports a par rate of exchange between its currency and that of the reserve center. A peripheral country may technically link its currency to gold instead of the reserve currency. For example, in 1969 Britain's pound was linked to gold at the fixed price of 14.58 pounds = 1 ounce. Since the U.S. dollar was tied to gold at the fixed price of $35 = 1 ounce, a par rate was established at $2.40 = £1 (i.e., $35/14.58 = $2.40). The line was rather artificial, because only the U.S. provided asset convertibility to foreign official institutions. Unlike the theoretical gold standard, in which the market rate was stabilized within the gold points due to the activities of profit motivated arbitragers, the market rate under the gold standard was to be officially maintained with a band around parity of plus/minus 1 percent. Should a country experience forces that push the market rate outside the band, its exchange stabilization fund must attempt to defend the band limits. However, if a "fundamental disequilibrium" occurs, a country's par rate may be redefined through expenditure-switching devaluations or revaluations. Diagrams 5-3 and 5-4 illustrate these points.

Diagram 5-3 represents the foreign exchange (i.e., Japanese yen) market in the U.S. Assuming a par rate between the dollar and the yen at R_0, the market rate could freely fluctuate within 1 percent around par value, shown by the band bounded by R_1 and R_2. Suppose an increase in U.S. incomes results in an increase in demand for Japanese exports, which induces the demand for

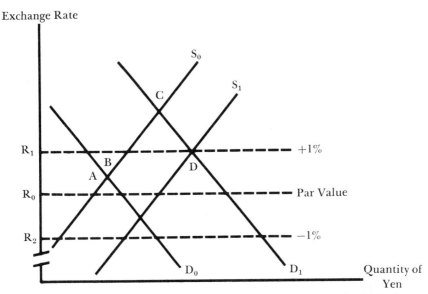

Exchange Rate

Diagram 5-3: *Exchange Rate Stabilization—Supporting the Dollar's Lower Limit*

yen to increase from D_0 to D_1. Under free market conditions, a new equilibrium would be established at point C; however, at this point the dollar would have depreciated by an amount greater than 1 percent. The U.S. exchange stabilization fund, which holds large quantities of foreign exchange, gold, and domestic currency, must intervene. At R_1 there is an excess demand for yen of quantity B-D. To keep the market rate from depreciating beyond R_1, the U.S. exchange stabilization fund uses its holdings of yen to finance the deficit; in effect the supply of yen increases from S_0 to S_1, therefore supporting the dollar's value within the band.

Diagram 5-4 illustrates the opposite case of a U.S. trade surplus with Japan. As the supply of yen increases from S_0 to S_1, under a free market system the dollar would appreciate from R_0 to the rate established at the new equilibrium point E. To keep the dollar from appreciating beyond R_2, the U.S. exchange stabilization fund using dollars purchases yen on the market by an amount equal to the payments surplus, F-G. This increases the demand for yen from D_0 to D_1, thus keeping the market rate within the band.

To the extent that an exchange stabilization fund defends the band, the supply and demand curves of foreign exchange become perfectly elastic at the upper and lower band limits. However, suppose that in Diagram 5-3 the U.S. external deficit of quantity B-D was viewed to be a "fundamental disequilibrium." In this case the U.S. exchange stabilization fund would not likely be willing to finance this irreversible deficit, for its reserves are limited; maintaining the dollar support price, R_1, over the long run will exhaust its reserve holdings. The U.S. may therefore devalue its currency with the hope that the ensuing depreciation will be sufficient to reverse the imbalance. *Ceteris paribus,* by increasing the dollar price of gold, the dollar would experience an across-the-board depreciation against all other currencies. However, if all other currencies were simultaneously devalued with the dollar by the same amount, there would be no depreciation or appreciation of any currency.

Under the IMF arrangements, the width of the band was determined by the central bankers' agreement to keep the spread within 1 percent on either side of par value with the dollar, a total spread of 2 percent. Prior to August, 1971, the members of the European Economic Community agreed not to utilize the full band width, but to restrict themselves to a 0.75 percent move-

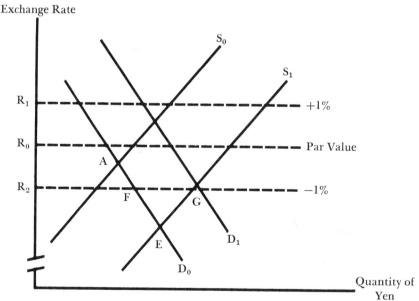

Diagram 5-4: Exchange Rate Stabilization—Maintaining the Dollar's Upper Limit

ment on either side of parity. Given this total spread, the cross rates between any two countries other than the U.S. as the reserve center could vary as much as 4 percent, while the value of the dollar with respect to any other currency could vary by no more than plus/minus 1 percent. Because the dollar was the de facto numeraire of the dollar-gold system, its spread was one-half that of peripheral countries' cross rates.

To see how the above works, assume two hypothetical exchange rates where the U.S. is the reserve center while Britain and West Germany are peripheral countries—1 mark = $1, and 1 pound = $3.[6] Allowing a band of plus/minus 1 percent around par value with the dollar, these ranges are established:

$$1 \text{ pound} = 300¢ \left\langle \begin{array}{l} 303¢ \\ 297¢ \end{array} \right. \quad \text{and } 1 \text{ mark} = 100¢ \left\langle \begin{array}{l} 101¢ \\ 99¢ \end{array} \right.$$

The cross rates between the mark and the pound fall within the range of:

Lower bound in terms of pound   Upper bound in terms of pound
297¢/101¢=2.94 marks/pound   303¢/99¢=3.06 marks/pound

Thus, the range is 0.12 mark. Using the midpoint of the range, 3 marks, as a base, the percent cross rate between the mark and the pound is 4 percent (i.e., 0.12/3 = .04). Although the value of the dollar with respect to either the mark or the pound could vary by no more than plus/minus 1 percent (i.e., a total spread of 2 percent), the potential cross rate between the mark and pound is 4 percent.

PROBLEMS OF THE DOLLAR-GOLD SYSTEM

Liquidity. Chapter 3 suggested that it is impossible to determine an optimal level of international reserves for the years ahead, for this level depends upon both objective and subjective criteria: the nature and strength of forces which create potential imbalances; the effectiveness of the adjustment mechanism to eliminate the disequilibrium; the quantity and quality of owned and borrowed reserves.

Since World War II, the principal sources of liquidity have been the growth of monetary gold stocks and deficits in the U.S.

balance of payments. Table 3-1 shows that gold as a component of IMF countries' reserves fell from 69 percent to 24.8 percent between 1950 and 1972, while foreign exchange, notably the dollar, rose from 27.6 percent to 64.9 percent. During the 1950s and 1960s it became evident that given the reluctance of countries to undergo significant internal and/or external adjustments, the need for liquidity to finance imbalances would increase as the volume of international transactions expanded. Because the growth of gold did not match the increase in demand for liquidity, the need for dollar reserves became evident. The dollar-gold system became known as a "disequilibrium system" due to the practice of the U.S. supplying liquidity for the world through its deficits.[7] This is illustrated in Diagram 5-5 below, which is based upon the assumptions and conclusions of Diagram 2-3.

Diagram 5-5 assumes that in order for the liquidity balance line LL to shift outward from L_1 toward L_2 and L_3, denoting higher combinations of U.S. and ROW incomes where the global demand and supply of liquidity equate, the U.S. must accept an

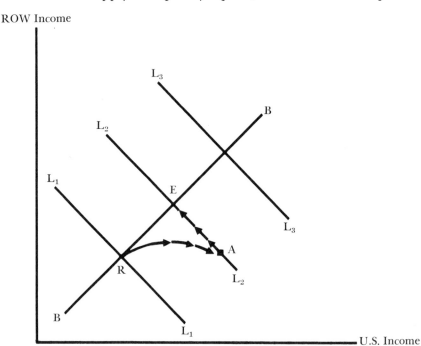

Diagram 5-5: Dollar-Gold Disequilibrium System

external deficit. Otherwise the growing need for liquidity would exceed the supply, implying a point to the right of any given liquidity balance line. A U.S. deficit with the ROW is shown by the rightward deviation from the external balance line BB. The dollar shortage of the early 1950s implied that the ROW welcomed the U.S. undergoing balance-of-payment deficits, shown by the movement from R to A. However, during the late 1960s and early 1970s, short- and long-run confidence problems developed, for U.S. gold reserves were rapidly deteriorating, which raised doubts about her ability to maintain asset convertibility.[8] It was often felt that the U.S. should reverse its external deficit with the ROW and move back toward line BB. But this would restrict the expansion of liquidity, for ROW currency did not serve as an international currency.

The dilemma of the disequilibrium nature of the dollar-gold system was that although the reduction or elimination of U.S. deficits would strengthen the dollar as a reserve currency, it would also cut off a major source of international currency. In a multi-asset system where the stock of monetary gold grows at a lesser rate than the demand for international money, the need for the reserve currency as a source of liquidity suggests falling reserve ratios of the reserve center, which may intensify the confidence problem. Therefore, the liquidity problem of the dollar-gold system involved dimensions of quality as well as the composition of reserve assets.

Adjustment Asymmetries. A first asymmetry of the dollar-gold system arose from the probability that a country with the smallest involvement in international transactions, measured in relation to its total economy, has a greater capacity to focus primary attention upon issues directly relating to its internal balance. This is because external imbalances will be of relatively less consequence upon a nation's level of output, employment, and income. During the 1960s, countries such as France criticized the U.S. for not practicing responsible financial discipline, largely because of its relatively insulated domestic economy. For countries more closely tied to international trade, external imbalances have greater repercussions upon their internal balances. During the late 1960s, exports as a percent of gross national product amounted to about 5 percent for the U.S., 13 percent for Britain, 18 percent for West Germany, 35 percent for Belgium, and 32 percent for the Netherlands.

A second asymmetry concerned the financing of external deficits. Because the dollar has been the major reserve currency, unlike peripheral countries the U.S. has not always lost reserves due to deficits. Rather, it has accumulated debts to foreign central banks through outstanding dollar liabilities. In effect, the U.S. had the privilege of transferring its deficits into a flow of real goods and services, called seigniorage. This transfer of resources accrued uniquely to the reserve center, for it was only through the peripheral countries' payment surpluses with the reserve center that they could increase their stocks of international currency. This unique privilege was attacked during the mid-1960s when France demanded the U.S. to fulfill its asset convertibility pledge by converting dollar holdings into gold.

A third asymmetry resulted from an expenditure-switching policy bias relating to surplus and deficit countries.[9] In contrast to monetary-fiscal expenditure-changing policies, which adjust the level of internal demand, expenditure-switching policies are designed to divert domestic and foreign expenditures between home and foreign products. These instruments include exchange rate adjustments, import controls such as quotas and tariffs, etc. Under the dollar-gold system, the surplus country left the bulk of the adjustment burden to the deficit country, for reserve losses were considered more critical than reserve gains. The ability of deficit countries to finance imbalances is restricted by their stocks of owned and borrowed reserves; also the capacity to neutralize reserve losses is limited. Under a pure gold-standard, in which deficit nations would obey the "rules of the game" and actively adopt contractionary expenditure-reducing monetary policies, a deflationary bias would exist due to the severity of the problems imposed by deficits. However, the desire to maintain internal balance under the dollar-gold system upon several occasions induced countries to resort to expenditure-switching policies rather than undergo substantial internal adjustments. Because it was easier and more politically acceptable to neutralize reserve inflows and postpone adjustments involving currency revaluations, the dollar-gold system had a devaluation bias.

A fourth asymmetry related to the degree of freedom of expenditure-switching devaluations/revaluations between the reserve center and peripheral countries.[10] Under the dollar-gold system, the dollar as the reserve currency had two ties: first, the tie with other currencies through a system of fixed exchange rates;

second, conversion rate between the dollar and all other currencies participating in the system since the dollar was the de facto numeraire. It was because the dollar served as an intervention currency and international denominator that the U.S. freedom to unilaterally change its exchange rate vis-à-vis currencies denominated in dollars was restricted. In contrast to peripheral countries that could unilaterally change their exchange rates, the dollar's rate was determined by foreign central banks intervening in the foreign exchange market with dollars.

With the U.S. dollar serving as an international standard of value, peripheral countries stood ready to buy and sell dollars in order to maintain their exchange rates with the dollar. However, this resulted in the U.S. losing control over its exchange rate.[11] The reason for this is that if there exist N countries with N currencies, there can be no more than N-1 independently determined exchange rates between these currencies, when one serves as the numeraire. If $N = 2$, and West Germany decides that 3 marks is the correct exchange rate for the dollar, the U.S. is prevented from simultaneously exchanging 2 marks for the dollar. When $N = 3$ or more, two countries like West Germany and France that use the dollar as a numeraire must maintain cross rates of exchange which are kept consistent by private arbitragers. The role of the numeraire currency makes its position asymmetrical with respect to other currencies, because to fix the price of other currencies in terms of the numeraire requires using the numeraire currency as a medium of intervention, vehicle of transactions, and store of value. The reserve center must therefore be passive with respect to determining the exchange rate of its currency; any change in its par value would disrupt the economies of all countries whose currencies are defined in terms of the reserve currency. The Nth currency problem implies that if each country has a distinct instrument (i.e., exchange rate policy) to control its external balance, there is an additional degree of freedom. Only N-1 independent balance-of-payments instruments are required in an N country world, since equilibrium in the balances of N-1 countries suggests equilibrium in the balance of the Nth country. The "redundancy problem" is the problem of deciding how to use the extra degree of freedom.[12] Under the dollar-gold system, the dollar served as the de facto numeraire; prior to 1971 it was generally felt that if the U.S. devalued the dollar, most other currencies would follow suit, thus preventing any actual change of exchange rates with respect to the dollar. A related aspect of this asymmetry was that because the dollar was the de facto numeraire and intervention currency, market rates involving the dollar could move only half as much as the cross rates between other currencies tied to the dollar. This problem was of minor consequence during the dollar-gold system era. However, with expanded bands around parity following the Smithsonian Agreements (i.e., plus/minus 2.25 percent), the potential spread between any two currencies other than the dollar was 9 percent.[13] Diagram 5-6 distinguishes between the legal and economic distinctions involving changing the par value of a currency. A devaluation in the legal sense refers to a country changing the official par value of its currency with respect to gold. A devaluation in the economic sense implies that a currency's value falls (i.e., depreciates) relative to that of another currency.

Diagram 5-6 denotes gold as the de jure numeraire by placing on the ordinate the price of dollars in terms of gold, and on the abscissa the price of pounds (i.e., representative of all other currencies of the world) in terms of gold. Each point in the graph represents three price ratios: the gold price of the dollar; the

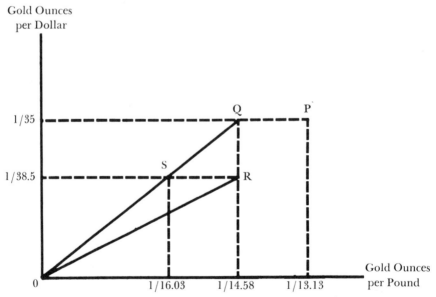

Diagram 5-6: *Legal and Economic Implications of Devaluation under the Dollar-Gold System*

gold price of the pound; the pound price of the dollar (i.e., the slope of the ray connecting a point from the origin to a point such as Q) and the dollar price of the pound (i.e., the reciprocal of the slope of the ray connecting the origin and any point in the graph.

Diagram 5-6 illustrates what is meant by a devaluation of the dollar. It could indicate a reduction in the gold price of the dollar (i.e., an increase in the dollar price of gold), the gold price of the pound remaining constant—a movement from Q toward R. It could indicate a uniform reduction of the gold price of both the dollar and the pound—a movement from Q toward S. It could also mean an increase in the dollar price of the pound (i.e., a revaluation of the pound with respect to gold while the gold price of the dollar remains constant)—a movement from Q toward P. Any change in the exchange rate between the dollar and the pound requires a change in the slope of the ray from the origin to a point on the graph.

Starting at Q, suppose a U.S. devaluation with respect to gold results in a movement from Q to R. Initially, the dollar depreciates with respect to the pound, shown by the slope of the ray OR. Now suppose that Britain retaliates by devaluing sterling, which induces a movement from R to S. Since S is on the initial ray, OQ, there has been no change in the dollar/pound exchange rate (i.e., no depreciation/appreciation of either currency with respect to the other).

A numerical example may help illustrate the above point. Assume initially that at Q, 1 ounce of gold = $35, and 1 ounce of gold = 14.58 pounds; the pound price of the dollar is 1 pound = $2.40 (i.e., $35/14.58 = $2.40). Now suppose that the U.S. devalues the dollar 10 percent with respect to gold—1 ounce of gold = $38.50—and that Britain devalues the pound 10 percent— 1 ounce of gold = 16.03 pounds. Although both currencies have been equally devalued with respect to gold, implying a movement from Q to S, their exchange rate still remains £1 = $2.40 (i.e., $38.50/16.03 = $2.40). Note that on the ordinate of Diagram 5-5 the gold price of the dollar falls when there is a movement towards the origin (i.e., 1/35 > 1/38.5). On the abscissa a movement towards the origin implies a reduction in the gold price of the pound (i.e., 1/14.58 > 1/16.03). This implies that when a currency is legally devalued with respect to gold, it does not necessarily result in a devaluation in the economic sense, for a change in the exchange rate requires the other country to refrain from undertaking an offsetting legal devaluation.[14]

The essence of the asymmetry relating to the degree of freedom in changing the exchange rate for the reserve center and peripheral countries is twofold. First, because the dollar served as an intervention currency and international denominator, the Nth currency problem suggested that all other countries together determined the U.S. exchange rate. Second, since all other countries stating their exchange rates in terms of the dollar would appreciate, should the U.S. unilaterally devalue the dollar with respect to gold, it was generally held that they would undergo offsetting devaluations.

Besides the U.S. not having control over its exchange rate under the dollar-gold system, most other countries generally were reluctant to use expenditure-switching policies. This lack of incentive to adjust was primarily due to institutional restraints, largely political in origin, which limited the degree of freedom in which the system could operate. Diagram 5-7 illustrates this point.

Diagram 5-7 applies to a two-country model, the U.S. and Jurope (i.e., the European Economic Community countries, notably West Germany, and Japan under the dollar-gold standard).[15] It makes the following assumptions. First, the vertical axis measures the external surplus or deficit per unit period of time, while the horizontal axis represents the extent of recession or inflation. In terms of the diagram, the vertical coordinates of one country are opposite in sign to and identical in quantity to the vertical coordinates of the other country; the reserve gain by one country is therefore identical to the reserve loss of the other. Second, the forms of expenditure-switching policies are limited to devaluations /revaluations. This is because the other major expenditure-switching instrument—import controls—has limited usefulness. At one extreme, import controls cannot be reduced below zero. At the other extreme, governments will not normally tighten import controls indefinitely. They are thus considered "non-linear" policies, and do not apply to the diagram, which is based upon "linear" policies that can be used indefinitely in either direction. A currency devaluation (i.e., depreciation) results in a northeasterly direction, while a revaluation (i.e., appreciation) results in a southwesterly direction. Also, a currency depreciation by one country implies an appreciation of the other's currency by the same amount, for in a two-country world there can be only one exchange rate. Third, any expenditure-switching policy undertaken by a country induces changes in both its vertical and horizontal coordinates. Whenever one country attempts to change its exchange rate, it disrupts the position of the other country. Fourth, both countries desire to attain external and internal balance, denoted by the point where the horizontal and vertical axes cross (i.e., the origin). This point of overall balance is largely politically determined, for each government has its own view on what constitutes internal balance. Last, any expenditure-switching policy undertaken by a country is primarily intended to reverse its external imbalance.

In this model it is assumed that the degree of freedom for one country to initiate expenditure-switching policies is the result of international negotiation. One reason for this assumption is

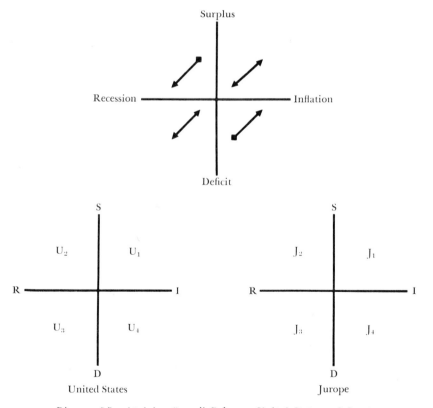

Diagram 5-7: Attaining Overall Balance—United States and Jurope

that in a two-country world there exists only one exchange rate. Also, changes in one country's external balance imply a disruption of the other country's payment position. Furthermore, an expenditure-switching policy undertaken by a country induces changes in both countries' internal and external sectors. Therefore, any proposal by one country to initiate an expenditure-switching policy implies that the other country must be willing to accept a change in its overall balance. The agreements concerning the direction and magnitude of the policy change may require implicit bargaining and perhaps strategies familiar to oligopoly theory. Table 5-1 summarizes the effects of the eight possible expenditure-switching policy combinations of Diagram 5-7 for

Table 5-1: Possible Exchange Rate Policy Combinations for External Balance—U.S. and Jurope

Situation	Possible Exchange Rate Policies	Effect
U_1-J_3	U.S. revaluation	U.S. moves toward overall balance
	Jurope devaluation	Jurope moves toward overall balance
U_1-J_4	U.S. revaluation	U.S. moves toward overall balance
	Jurope devaluation	Jurope inflation intensified
U_2-J_3	U.S. revaluation	U.S. recession intensified
	Jurope devaluation	Jurope moves toward overall balance
U_2-J_4	U.S. revaluation	U.S. recession intensified
	Jurope devaluation	Jurope inflation intensified
U_3-J_1	U.S. devaluation	U.S. moves toward overall balance
	Jurope revaluation	Jurope moves toward overall balance
U_3-J_2	U.S. devaluation	U.S. moves toward overall balance
	Jurope revaluation	Jurope recession intensified
U_4-J_1	U.S. devaluation	U.S. inflation intensified
	Jurope revaluation	Jurope moves toward overall balance
U_4-J_2	U.S. devaluation	U.S. inflation intensified
	Jurope revaluation	Jurope recession intensified

attaining mutual external balance for the U.S. and Jurope. In Diagram 5-7 there can be only eight possible policy combinations between the two countries, because if one has a surplus it implies that the other must have a deficit. Therefore, their points of location must be on the opposite sides of their respective horizontal axes, each by the same distance only in opposite sign.[16]

Suppose the U.S. and Jurope are initially located at points U_3 and J_1 respectively in Diagram 5-7. The U.S. would find it advantageous to propose a dollar devaluation (i.e., depreciation) to reduce her external deficit. Jurope would find it beneficial to have its currency appreciate against the dollar to reverse her external surplus. Although primarily aimed at combating an external imbalance, Jurope's appreciation would also tend to reverse her economy's expansion and inflationary pressures. This is because the appreciation would reduce net exports which, through the multiplier, would reduce the inflationary pressures. At the same time, the opposite forces would tend to reduce the U.S. recession. In this case the U.S. depreciation and Jurope appreciation would be beneficial to both countries from the perspective of eliminating their external and internal disequilibriums, hence promoting mutual overall balance. Any policy negotiations would likely include issues relating to the magnitude and timing of the expenditure switching policy.

Now suppose that the U.S. and Jurope are initially located at points U_4 and J_2 respectively. In this situation there would be no possible exchange rate policy combination that would be desirable to both countries. A U.S. depreciation and Jurope appreciation could achieve the primary objective of reserving both countries' external imbalances, but the induced repercussions upon their internal sectors would likely be politically unacceptable. Because the dollar depreciation would result in a north-easterly movement on the diagram, the cost of eliminating the U.S. payment would be a larger inflation. And since the Juropean currency's appreciation induced a southwesterly movement on the diagram, to combat its external surplus Jurope would have to accept a greater recession. This expenditure-switching policy combination for combating the external imbalance would be unacceptable to both countries due to the undesirable costs that it imposes on their respective internal balances. This case therefore presents an exchange rate policy dilemma for both countries, for the secondary effects of the U.S. depreciation and Jurope appreciation would induce adverse effects on both countries' internal sectors that would prevent either of them from moving toward overall balance.

Besides the use of expenditure-switching policies to restore overall balance, stabilization may require monetary and fiscal expansionary or contractionary policies. The implications of these policies are illustrated in Diagram 5-8, a modification of Diagram 5-7.[17] The diagram indicates that both monetary and fiscal expenditure-reducing and expenditure-increasing policies result in northwesterly and southeasterly movements along MM and FF respectively, which show the direction of change that these policies must take to reverse internal and/or external imbalances. The slopes of MM and FF depend upon the propensity to consume, the propensity to import, the interest elasticity of the liquidity preference and investment, and the tax structure. The MM function is steeper than the FF function because the sensitivity of external balance is greater to monetary policy changes than to those of fiscal policy; that is, the monetary change required to induce a given change in the balance of payments is less than that of fiscal policy.[18] This is illustrated below.

Expenditure-Reducing/
Increasing Policy by
Monetary Means

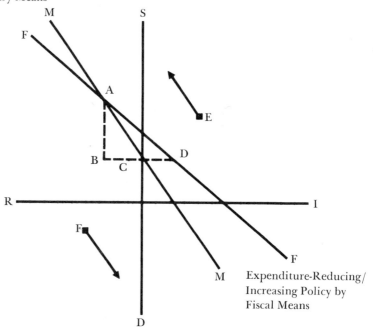

Expenditure-Reducing/
Increasing Policy by
Fiscal Means

Diagram 5-8: Interaction of Monetary and Fiscal Expenditure Changing Policies for a Single Nation

In the second quadrant of Diagram 5-8, as expansionary monetary policy is undertaken to reverse the overall imbalance, not only will the external surplus be reduced due to rising imports, but there will be some capital outflows induced by the yield differential. The capital flow and trade effects of monetary policy on external balance are thus mutually reinforcing. However, an expansionary fiscal policy will be accompanied by some potential capital inflows, due to the rising transaction demand for money that induces higher interest rates, thus offsetting part of the reduction in the deteriorating trade balance. The trade and capital flow effects on the balance of payments of fiscal policy are therefore offsetting. For the same reduction in an external surplus, the fiscal policy must be more expansionary than the monetary policy. In terms of the diagram, if a country chose to reduce its balance-of-payment surplus by amount AB, this would require a monetary expansion of BC, or a fiscal expansion of BD, provided that each policy was used independently. The amount of required fiscal change thus exceeds that of monetary policy by CD.

As long as a country faces either a surplus with recession or an inflation with a deficit, the effects of monetary and fiscal expenditure-changing policies are consistent with each other in that they harmoniously restore overall balance. However, if a country faces either a surplus with inflation or a recession with a deficit, any combination of policies to combat one form of disequilibrium will aggravate the other. For instance, suppose a country is initially located at point E, at which there is a surplus with inflation. To reduce aggregate spending, the monetary authorities would tighten credit; but this would likely result in net capital inflows induced by higher interest rates. At the same time fiscal restraint would result in reduced government spending to halt inflation; however, as income falls import purchases decrease. Although these expenditure-reducing policies would move point E toward internal balance (i.e., the vertical axis), it would be prevented from moving inward toward the origin, the point of overall balance. Now suppose that a country is located at point F, where there exists a recession and deficit. Any effort to combat the recession through expansionary monetary and fiscal policies would aggravate the deficit; easing credit that results in falling interest rates may induce net capital outflows, while higher levels of government spending that result in rising incomes may spur increasing imports. Thus point F would be prevented from moving to the origin, the point of overall balance. Given the two regions of conflicting policies, it is possible that overall balance could be attained by manipulating the two policy variables so that the positive response to a given policy in one area (i.e., monetary policy for external balance—fiscal policy for internal balance) exceeds the negative response in the other. However, this would imply costly internal adjustments over a long period of time in the form of alternating bouts of recession and inflation.

This discussion suggests that given relatively small internal and external disturbances which can be effectively combated by monetary and fiscal expenditure-changing policies, the need for expenditure-switching policies declines. However, should external imbalances be so large that their correction requires excessive internal adjustments in output, employment, and income, the need for expenditure-switching devaluations/revaluations may arise. Based upon the assumptions and conclusions of Diagram 5-7 and Diagram 5-8, the following analysis illustrates this point for the U.S. and Jurope under the dollar-gold system.

Diagram 5-9 suggests that because only one exchange rate exists between the U.S. and Jurope, political realities imply that these countries will agree, whether informally or formally, to refrain from using unlimited devaluations/revaluations. This implies that each country determines the extent to which external disequilibrium can exist before it must resort to expenditure-switching measures. If located within these politically determined tolerance boundaries, suggesting that the imbalance is perceived to be a short-run problem, a country would combat a disequilibrium through expenditure-changing policies. However, if located outside the boundary, which implies intolerable imbalances of "fundamental disequilibrium" magnitude, the restoration of external balance requires expenditure-switching devalutions or revaluations.

Diagram 5-9 illustrates how the above boundaries of tolerance for the U.S. and Jurope under the dollar-gold system led to relatively stable exchange rates. The dimensions of the U.S. boundary, abcd, differs from that of Jurope, efgh, for several reasons. First, the need for liquidity during the 1960s resulted in the U.S. supplying reserves via external deficits; in terms of the diagram, this suggests that the U.S. agreed to tolerate a greater deficit and a smaller surplus than Jurope. Because Jurope was a peripheral country, it was afraid to stop accumulating reserves through payment surpluses, since it did not have the privilege of its currency liabilities being considered international money. Second, Jurope has traditionally accepted higher rates of inflation, while the U.S. has tolerated larger levels of unemployment.

Within the U.S. and Juropean boundaries, there exists a smaller area of mutually tolerable external and internal disequilibriums, denoted by eicj. This area illustrates conceptually the exchange rate stability between the U.S. and Jurope during the 1960s. During the early 1960s, the U.S. faced a deficit with recession, point U_1, while Jurope experienced a surplus with inflation, point J_1. Since these disequilibriums were mutually regarded as minor disturbances, the countries refrained from using expenditure-switching policies and instead resorted to monetary and fiscal measures. By 1970 the U.S. had moved from U_1 to U_2, denoting

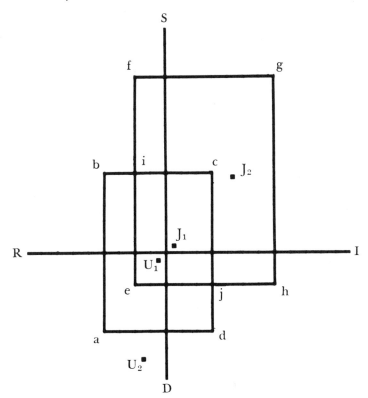

Diagram 5-9: Political Acceptance of Expenditure-Changing/Expenditure-Switching Policies

an inflation with deficit, while Jurope's inflation and surplus position moved from J_1 to J_2. This situation was viewed as intolerable by the U.S. since it was located outside the boundary of acceptable deviations from overall balance. At the same time Jurope remained within her acceptable boundary, reflecting the asymmetry between surplus and deficit countries whereby the pressure to adjust was faced primarily by the latter. By the early 1970s the U.S. viewed this situation as a "fundamental disequilibrium" that could only be resolved by allowing the overvalued dollar to depreciate against Jurope's currencies, notably the yen and West Germany's mark.

External Currency Market

Throughout the late 1960s and 1970s, a primary source of external transactions has come from the rise of U.S. dollar deposits in financial centers outside the U.S., and of mark deposits in centers outside West Germany. Among the traditional financial centers are London, Singapore, and Zurich. However, with the advent of the 1973–74 energy crisis, the Arab nations have become important holders of dollar and mark deposits. The primary feature of an external currency market is that commercial banks accept interest-bearing deposits denominated in currencies other than those of the country in which they are located, and then relend these funds either in that same currency, in the currency of the country in which they operate, or in a third country's currency.[19] Although there currently exists viable currency markets in Asia, Europe, and in the Arab countries—respectively called Asian-currency, Euro-currency, and Petro-currency markets —this section will concentrate on the Eurodollar market. This is because the Eurodollar market has been the primary market for external currency flows of the major industrial nations.

The purpose of the Eurodollar market, with its financial center in London, has been to provide a market with no national boundaries, where short-term capital can be mobilized on a global basis for borrowers and investors. The banks that produce the external currency deposits are termed Eurobanks. Currently, there are several hundred Eurobanks that issue external currency deposits upon investor demand. For the majority of these banks, Eurodollar transactions are of secondary importance to their primary activities as domestic banks. However, for many of the largest foreign branches of U.S. banks, such as Chase Manhattan and Bank of America, Eurocurrency transactions are their primary activity.

Development of the Eurodollar Market. Eurodollars are essentially deposit liabilities, denominated in dollars, of banks outside the United States. However, it was not until the late 1950s that the market began to gain prominence as a major source of short-term capital. Several factors have led to the Eurodollar market's development.[20] First, for political reasons, the Eastern European countries, notably Russia, following World War II preferred to hold their U.S. dollar balances in European banks rather than in the U.S. This was because during World War II the U.S. had impounded Russian dollar holdings in the U.S. Russia thus desired dollar holdings that were free from U.S. government regulation. A second reason was the initiation of Regulation Q by the Federal Reserve during the late 1950s, whereby U.S. commercial banks were effectively limited in the amount of interest that they could pay on time deposits. When this interest rate ceiling was reached, dollar flows moved into Eurodollar deposits that generally paid higher interest rates—this activity promoted an expanding Eurodollar market. A third inducement was the U.S. initiation during the late 1960s of exchange controls designed to reverse the U.S. external deficit. However, these measures paradoxically led to the growth of greater external deposits. For instance, in 1965 the U.S. adopted voluntary controls on U.S. lending abroad and on foreign investment. As a result, foreign investors increased their demand for external dollars in the Eurodollar market. This induced higher Eurodollar interest rates, which stimulated a greater flow of funds out of the U.S. to London.

Although the above factors help explain the historical development of the Eurodollar market, its main significance is that Eurobanks, like domestic commercial banks, are part of a fractional reserve banking system. Therefore, the great volume of Eurodollars is largely the result of the multiple deposit expansion that occurs under fractional reserve banking. This process yields an inverted pyramiding of credit for international investors. Eurodollar deposits are created when persons transfer deposits from banks in the U.S. to a Eurobank. The example below illustrates the creation of Euro-deposits.[21]

Assume that an international investor decides to transfer his deposit from a New York bank to a London bank. When the London bank receives the investor's check, suppose it deposits it in its account in a U.S. bank. At this point the total deposits of the U.S. banks have remained constant, since the investor's deposit withdrawal was precisely offset by the increase of the London bank deposit at its U.S. bank. However, for the world as a whole, there has been an increase in dollar deposits—the volume of deposits in London has increased, while that in the U.S. is unchanged. The second step in the Euro-deposit creation process occurs when the London bank makes a loan to its customers; by increasing the customer's demand deposit account in exchange for his promissory note, new Eurodollar deposits are created. Therefore, each dollar deposit transferred from a U.S. bank to a Eurobank can support a multiple expansion of deposits, depending on the banking regulations that exist in the Eurobank's respective countries. In practice, Eurobanks have not been subject to required reserve regulations, although prudent bank management suggests a minimal safety reserve cushion.

Significance of the Eurodollar Market. A beneficial aspect of the Eurodollar market is its international nature and freedom from regulation of a given country, which promotes the mobilization of short-term capital and its global distribution as dictated by international supply and demand. However, there exist several other economic effects.

The primary effect of the Eurodollar market has been the expansion of short-term capital flows which are induced by interest rate differentials among financial centers. However, these flows have increased the financial interdependence of the countries involved in the market, the result being that countries are less able to pursue an independent domestic monetary policy under a system of pegged exchange rates. Another impact of the Eurodollar market is its effect on the foreign exchange market. Although the volume of Eurodollar transactions is substantial, only a portion of them directly affect market exchange rates. To affect market rates, these transactions must involve the conversion of a domestic currency into Eurodollars, or vice versa. Hence, there is no direct effect if Eurodollars flow out of or into a country in the form of U.S. dollars. However, the conversion of Eurodollars into other currencies induces downward pressure on the

U.S. market rate, while strengthening the rates of other currencies.[22]

As verified in the international currency crises of 1971 and 1973, the effects of destabilizing capital flows on exchange rates are substantial. And with the pyramiding of short-term credit that exists under the fractional Euro-deposit expansion system, the role of the Eurodollar is an important source of international credit. With the global interdependence of monetary and exchange rate policies that currently exists, there is a need for the international regulation of the Eurodollar market system. What has worried central bankers is that the growth of Eurodollars has primarily been attributed to the Euro-deposit multiple expansion process, in which an inverted pyramid of credit results. It has been feared that a destabilizing shock to the international monetary system might be sufficient to topple the entire pyramid of Eurodollar credit. And with the monetary regulations of countries differing, it is possible for interest-induced, short-term capital flows to circumvent domestic monetary regulation. This was seen in the capital flow movements of the late 1960s and 1970s.

As will later be discussed, throughout 1974 and 1975 the Euro-currency market was buffeted and rocked by the following factors: global inflation; the failures of several large, prestigious banks in the United States and West Germany; the massive balance-of-payments deficits of the oil-importing countries; the erratic currency exchange rate movements under the managed floating system. Yet in spite of these destabilizing forces, the Euro-currency market continued to survive and grow. Part of the reason for this is that the central bankers of the major financial countries in 1975 took limited steps to preserve confidence in the Eurobanks. The major central banks of Europe, Japan, and the United States publicly reassured the Eurobanks that they will stand ready as a "lender of last resort" in case of financial emergency. However, this is not a blanket guarantee—in return for this support the Eurobanks are expected to manage their operations soundly and refrain from making risky loans or engaging in other questionable practices.

THE INTERNATIONAL MONETARY CRISES OF 1971–1973

August 15, 1971—The Dollar Standard. Throughout the

1960s, it became evident that the dollar-gold standard suffered from three basic flaws. First, a deterioration of confidence in the dollar as a reserve currency resulted in speculation against it and the demands of foreign central bankers, notably the French, that the U.S. live up to her asset convertibility pledge by converting outstanding dollar liabilities into gold. A second flaw was a liquidity problem, which stemmed from the fact that a growing use of the dollar as a reserve asset suggested both expanding U.S. deficits and falling reserve ratios of gold assets to foreign-held dollar obligations. It was obvious that neither of these practices could continue without intensifying a confidence problem. Third, an adjustment problem existed; not only did other countries lack the initiative to change their official par values, largely due to feelings that this would lower world respect for their ability to maintain financial discipline, but with the dollar as an intervention currency the U.S. did not have the ability of peripheral countries to change its exchange rate against all other currencies as a whole. Therefore, the system suffered significant rigidities and asymmetries in its adjustment mechanism.[23]

When domestic inflation intensified during the late 1960s in the U.S., the dollar gradually became an overvalued currency, and U.S. export and import-competing industries suffered. With the exception of West Germany, countries that found their currencies undervalued refused to appreciate. Proper adjustment called for a U.S. depreciation. However, under the dollar-gold system, the U.S. lacked the ability to do so. The only unilateral action left to the U.S. was to suspend the asset convertibility of the dollar; this allowed the dollar to float in the international money markets, and created incentives for exchange rate changes. As a result, the dollar-gold system was terminated, and a pure dollar-standard was born; U.S. deficits would now solely be settled by dollar liabilities rather than gold. Although gold still served as the other reserve asset held by central banks, without the U.S. supporting the price of gold as the residual supplier, gold represented an untradable asset. The other component of official reserves, SDRs, was of minor importance in 1971.[24]

The Smithsonian Agreements. Besides the protection of its dwindling stock of gold reserves, a major goal of the U.S. suspension of the dollar's convertibility into gold was to let its exchange rate depreciate against the undervalued currencies—notably Japan's yen and West Germany's mark—according to the free market forces of supply and demand. Note that although it was thought the dollar would depreciate against most other major currencies, there was no official devaluation. This was because the dollar's de jure peg was still defined at $35 an ounce. Commonly mentioned objectives included a 12–15 percent appreciation of the yen and an 8 percent rise in the value of the mark against the dollar.

In spite of the floating of the dollar, the U.S. objectives were not achieved in the ensuing months. This was because the necessary condition for a dollar depreciation—a free market adjustment mechanism—did not exist. Rather, foreign governments prevented the exchange market from fully responding to supply and demand forces through their exchange market interventions. In managing an exchange rate a central banker that observes his currency's rate floating downward or upward steps into the market and buys his currency to prevent a depreciation or sells his currency to prevent an appreciation. How much he buys or sells and where he can obtain credit to do his buying determine the extent of exchange market intervention. The practice of central bankers controlling exchange rate movements through their exchange market operations is known as "managed" exchange rate system. Central bank exchange market operations is one method of conducting a managed float. There also exists a two-tier exchange mechanism, commonly referred to as a dual exchange rate system. This point will be discussed later.

Immediately after the August 15, 1971, floating of the overvalued dollar, Japan's central bank refused to allow the dollar's depreciation against the yen by trading yen for dollars on the exchange market. From the U.S. perspective, this was a "dirty float," whereby foreign central banking operations prevented the dollar's exchange rate from depreciating according to free market forces. Largely because of the managed floats practiced by Japan as well as several European countries, the U.S. dollar remained an overvalued currency in the last quarter of 1971. By December it was evident that the overvalued dollar would have to depreciate against most currencies of its trading partners. Rather than permitting the dollar to decrease in value under a system of freely floating exchange rates, foreign governments demanded a formal dollar devaluation in return for the termination of their interventions in the exchange market.

A dollar devaluation was demanded by foreign governments

for several reasons. First, it represented a political concession to Europe that the U.S. was guilty of not being able to maintain financial discipline and defend the dollar's international value. Second, gold-hoarding nations like France would potentially benefit from the U.S. increasing the official gold price. Third, unlike a system of floating rates, whereby the dollar maintains a separate exchange rate with each country, a U.S. devaluation implied an "across the board" depreciation against all foreign currencies that were not devalued with respect to gold or floated downward with the dollar. This was a major concession to Japan, whose currency was greatly undervalued with respect to the dollar. Japan contended that the burden of adjustment against the dollar should be shared more equitably by the major trading partners of the U.S., rather than having Japan undergo disproportionate appreciations against the dollar.

At the historic Smithsonian Agreements, announced on December 18, 1971, the U.S. yielded to foreign pressures and agreed to adjust its long-standing parity by increasing the dollar price of gold from $35 to $38 per ounce, a rise of 8.57 percent. This decreased the value of the dollar in terms of foreign currency by 7.89 percent. Mathematically, $38 exceeds $35 by 8.57 percent, but $35 is less than $38 by 7.89 percent. Other aspects of the agreement included removing the 10 percent import surtax imposed by the U.S. on August 15, 1971, and widening the bands around parity from plus/minus 1 percent to plus/minus 2.25 percent.

In return for the U.S. devaluation and removal of the import surtax, the nine other nations of the Group of Ten agreed to undergo a realignment of their exchange rates with the dollar. Table 5-2 summarizes these realignments whereby a new exchange rate structure emerged in roughly four categories. First, there were several countries, notably France and the United Kingdom, that held their existing official parities; these currencies in effect appreciated relative to the dollar by the full amount of the U.S. 8.57 percent devaluation. Second, several countries, including Japan, West Germany, the Netherlands, and Belgium, agreed to revalue their currencies with respect to gold in addition to the U.S. devaluation; this resulted in their currencies appreciating against the dollar by an amount greater than the U.S. devaluation. Third, a few countries, notably Sweden and Italy, devalued their currencies by about 1 percent, thus appreciating approximately

Table 5-2: Changes in Exchange Rates of Major Currencies against the U.S. Dollar: January 1, 1971, to December 31, 1971

Currency	Units per U.S. $ (Jan., 1971)	Units per U.S. $ (Dec., 1971)	Percent Change in Terms of U.S. $
Japanese yen	360.00	308.00	16.88
West German mark	3.66	3.22	13.58
Netherlands guilder	3.62	3.24	11.57
Belgian franc	50.00	44.82	11.57
French franc	5.55	5.12	8.57
United Kingdom pound	0.42	0.38	8.57
Swedish krona	5.17	4.81	7.49
Italian lira	625.00	581.50	7.48
Canadian dollar*	1.01	1.00	1.00

* Because Canada maintained a system of floating exchange rates, it did not adjust its parity.

Source: International Monetary Fund, *International Financial Statistics* (November, 1973), pp. 2–3.

7.5 percent against the dollar. Last, Canada did not undergo an official parity adjustment, but rather allowed her currency to float in the exchange market.

Crisis of 1973. The initial predictions about the U.S. devaluation were quite optimistic. It was estimated that the devaluation would bring an average depreciation of the dollar by 12 percent relative to the currencies of the Group of Ten countries, except Canada whose dollar floated along with the U.S. dollar. Several events stimulated confidence in the dollar during the first three quarters of 1972: the sterling crisis of June, 1972, which led to a float of Britain's pound; the August, 1972, increase of U.S. interest rates; and the expectations that the U.S. could halt its rate of inflation while Jurope's inflation was increasing. However, a number of factors led to adverse pressures on the dollar by January, 1973: renewed fears concerning the U.S. inability to cure its inflation; the introduction of a managed float by Italy, who adopted a two-tier market for its weakening lira; the floating of the Swiss franc; the U.S. announcement of its balance-of-payments statistics, which revealed a 1972 trade deficit of $6.4 billion and a payments deficit of $10.8 billion; the release of West German statistics which indicated a substantial increase in its balance-of-payments surplus during 1972; the February interventions by the U.S. and West German monetary authorities in the foreign exchange market to prevent the mark from appreciating outside of the Smithsonian band; the ensuing demand by Wilbur Mills, Chairman of the House Ways and Means Committee, that the U.S. again devalue its overvalued currency.

These events touched off a speculative crisis in which speculators fled from the weakening dollar into the undervalued yen and West German mark. To defend the Smithsonian bands, West Germany and Japan purchased some $6 billion and $1.6 billion respectively in the first days of February. After several days of negotiation, on February 12 the U.S. agreed to devalue the dollar 10 percent by increasing the price of gold from $38 to $42.22 per ounce. When the U.S. increased the price of gold by $4.22 per ounce, this amounted to a 10 percent dollar devaluation (i.e., $4.22/$42.22). Figured another way, the price of foreign currencies in terms of the dollar had risen approximately 11.1 percent. To illustrate, a West German would have to pay 10 percent fewer marks to buy a given number of dollars, but an American would have to exchange 11.1 percent more dollars for a given number of marks. This is because, before the devaluation, the mark's exchange rate was 3.22 to the dollar; after the devaluation, it was 2.90 marks per dollar. This implies that 2.90 is 10 percent less than 3.22 (i.e., 0.32/3.22), but 3.22 is 11.1 percent greater than 2.90 (i.e., 0.32/2.90).

Within the following week after the second U.S. devaluation, the following world exchange rate structure emerged. The dollar depreciated 10 percent against other currencies whose governments did not change their parities; included were the West German mark, French franc, Dutch guilder, and British pound. It depreciated more than 10 percent against Japan's floating yen, which rose nearly 17 percent in value relative to the dollar (i.e., approximately 10 percent because of the devaluation and 7 percent due to the float). Currencies that were devalued by an amount less than 10 percent found their values rising relative to the dollar; for instance, Sweden underwent a 5.5 percent appreciation against the dollar. The dollar's exchange rate did not change against currencies that were also devalued 10 percent; these nations, including Mexico, Israel, and South Korea, generally have largely depended on U.S. tourism, investment, and trade.[25]

In spite of the new world exchange rate realignments, the speculative attack continued into March and resulted in the termination of the Smithsonian bands. Japan continued a managed float of the yen, while the currencies of the European Economic Community jointly floated against the dollar. These policies destroyed the Smithsonian Agreements.

Although it was felt that the second U.S. devaluation would result in a sufficient decline in U.S. international prices, by May and June of 1973 doubts were arising over whether the February devaluation was a case of overkill and whether the dollar was evolving into an undervalued currency. Because of clerical error, the original estimate of the December U.S. trade deficit was vastly overstated, and the February devaluation occurred before the January statistics, which would have revealed a lower deficit than that of December, were announced.[26] This raises doubts whether the additional devaluation would have been as much as 10 percent had accurate data been available. Induced by two devaluations and a currency float, the U.S. trade balance improved from an $833 million deficit in the first quarter of 1973 to a surplus of $23 million in the second quarter and a $963 million surplus in the third quarter.[27]

The above figures raise questions concerning the nature of a currency devaluation. One explanation relates to the short- and long-run aspects of devaluation; this is called the J-curve effect. According to this theory, the effect of a devaluation upon a country's trade balance can be plotted on a J-curve. Immediately following a devaluation, a country's trade balance will deteriorate (i.e., a movement down the hook of the J); over the long run, an improvement (i.e., a movement up the J's stem) will normally occur).[28]

The J-curve effect assumes that in the short run the initial effects of a devaluation is an increase in import expenditures, for the volume is unchanged while the domestic import prices have risen. Only after a substantial period of time—the British 1967 devaluation suggested nearly two years—will the higher prices begin to slow import purchases while lower export prices to foreigners induce rising sales abroad. The lag between devaluation-induced changes in international prices and their ultimate effects on the trade balance can be attributed to several lags: in recognizing the new situation, in the decision to change real variables, in delivery time, in the replacement of inventories and materials, and in production.[29] This suggests that the initial effects of devaluation relate to price, while quantity adjustments occur only after substantial lags.

To the extent that the J-curve effect is valid, one would expect the Smithsonian devaluation to produce substantial improvement in the U.S. payments position within the ensuing one to two years. However, for several reasons U.S. policymakers questioned whether the first devaluation would prove effective. First, rising levels of domestic activity in the U.S. relative to that abroad during 1972 strengthened the U.S. role as a net importer, thus counteracting any favorable effects of the devaluation. Second, 1972 witnessed many foreign exporters to the U.S. offsetting the currency adjustment by lowering their prices and thus their profit margins to keep their products competitive to U.S. consumers. Third, it was questioned whether the demand elasticities for U.S. exports were so low that the initial devaluation price effects were insufficient to induce substantial responses in foreign demand. Because of these fears, and perhaps due to inadequate balance-of-payments statistics, the international monetary crisis of February, 1973, was sufficient to convince U.S. policymakers to undergo a second evaluation.

This chapter has discussed the dollar-gold system that existed from the early 1950s until August 15, 1971. Several objectives of a successful international payments mechanism were included in assessing the merits of this system: whether external imbalances are excessively large or prolonged; whether the correction of external disequilibriums requires costly internal adjustments in output, employment, and income; whether the system is conducive to expanding levels of international trade, finance, and investment.

It was found that although these goals generally were adequately fulfilled, during the 1960s it became apparent that the system suffered from several critical asymmetries and rigidities. Among these were the devaluation bias placed upon deficit countries, the inability of the reserve center to adjust its exchange rate with the same degree of freedom as peripheral countries, and the lack of incentive for disequilibrium peripheral countries to adjust via expenditure-switching policies.

The monetary crises of the late 1960s and 1971 put undue pressure on the U.S. pledge to maintain asset convertibility of the dollar. As a result, the dollar-gold system was terminated on

August 15, 1971. The subsequent dollar standard enhanced the U.S. ability and foreign central bankers' willingness to adjust their exchange rates, as seen in the dollar devaluations of 1971 and 1973, sterling's devaluation of 1972, the revaluations of Japan's yen and West Germany's mark, and the European Economic Community's joint float of 1973.

CHAPTER 6

Reforming the International Monetary System

INTRODUCTION

As discussed earlier, how well an international payments mechanism functions relates to the extent to which it can promote a politically acceptable international equilibrium without imposing excessive or prolonged costs upon disequilibrium nations. The dollar-gold system faced three major problems—liquidity, confidence, and adjustment. Any reform proposal concerning artificially stabilized exchange rates must include policies for dealing with these issues, for they determine the payment mechanism's capacity to function.

This chapter will discuss several reforms of and alternatives to the dollar-gold system. The first group of reform proposals relates to the feasibility of replacing and/or supplementing the system's existing reserve assets; primary emphasis is placed upon the issues of liquidity and confidence. The second group deals with how to improve the adjustment mechanism through exchange rate policies.

PROBLEMS OF A NEW INTERNATIONAL MONEY

Gresham's Law. During the early 1800s, the U.S. witnessed a period of bimetallism, whereby gold and silver coins circulated domestically at a legal ratio of 1 ounce of gold = 15 ounces of silver. However, on the world markets the price of gold was nearly 15.3 times the price of silver. Silver was therefore overvalued and gold was undervalued at the U.S. mint. In the sixteenth century Sir Thomas Gresham, master of England's mint, formulated a principle relating to the existence of two or more kinds of money of unequal exchange value in concurrent circulation. According to Gresham's Law, the overvalued money drives the undervalued money out of circulation. Rather than using gold in domestic transactions at the legal ratio of 15:1, it would pay to hoard gold or export it to places where its market value was recognized; silver would thus circulate on the domestic market.

Gresham's Law applies to any international financial arrangement which uses several assets for reserves. Since it basically involves dimensions of confidence and stability in the values of reserve assets, there may be problems in keeping all assets in circulation when the rate of exchange is fixed by the international monetary authority.[1] A basic flaw of the dollar-gold system was that international dollars were treated by their holders as second-class assets, for they largely derived their prestige from their asset convertibility into gold, the first-class asset. As the U.S. gold/dollar obligation reserve ratio fell during the 1960s, a confidence problem arose which resulted in doubts about the U.S. ability to maintain the stability of the dollar's convertibility.

Any proposal involving the creation of additional reserve assets must provide controls for their growth rates, specify the means of introducing the new assets into the system, and provide arrangements to assure that the new assets will be a first-class money, secure from depreciation against other reserve assets. Among the policies that could be initiated to fulfill these conditions are the following: first, a guarantee of the new asset's value in terms of gold, but with limited conversion privileges; second, an agreement among member nations to maintain no less than a given percent of their reserves in the new asset, as against gold; third, an efficient payments mechanism for the new asset; fourth, interest payments on holdings of the reserve asset; fifth, restriction of the use of national currencies as international reserves; sixth, a specific rule for the creation of the new asset; and seventh, a truly international new asset that is symmetrical in operation to the other assets, thus avoiding the asymmetries of the dollar-gold system.[2]

Seigniorage. A second problem involving the creation of a new form of international money involves the distribution of seigniorage. Originally, seigniorage referred to the difference between the circulating value of a coin and the cost of bullion and minting; this implied a once-and-for-all gain to the issuer. The term was later extended to international money by including the value of real goods and services accruing to the issuer of money due to the fact that money's face value exceeded the cost of producing and servicing it. Under the dollar-gold system, the U.S. as the reserve center had the unique privilege of receiving real goods and services for its cumulative external deficits. In effect, the peripheral countries granted the U.S. free credit, for it had no explicit obligation to repay the world its forgone real national absorption of goods and services. The U.S. benefited in two ways from its seigniorage. First, there was a current gain of real factors made available by its cumulative external deficit; this current gain ceases to accrue as soon as foreigners refuse to convert real resources into monetary deficits. Second, there was a capital benefit, which is the yield on the additional investment of the real resources made possible through external deficits.[3]

The amount of seigniorage available to a country whose currency is used as international money depends essentially on the extent of that country's monopoly position as a source of international currency. A country which has the monopoly power of issuing international money can experience large seigniorage benefits. But if it faces competition, in that several national currencies serve as international money, the amount of its seigniorage will fall. This is because it must now pay interest to induce foreigners to hold its currency obligations; as the degree of competition intensifies, higher interest rates must be paid. This suggests that for long-run seigniorage benefits to exist, imperfect competition must exist in the issuing of international currency.[4]

Because the cost of issuing currency is virtually zero, the potential value of seigniorage is substantial. Proposals to create new forms of international money face the problem of how the seigniorage gains should be distributed among the participating countries. There are three basic methods of distributing these gains.[5] First, there is a free market solution in which the issuing agency or country pays interest to the holders of its currency. A second method is a central government solution involving the authorities using real resources acquired from the issuance of money to acquire public goods which could be used for such projects as aiding the less developed countries or redistributing income among nations. Third, a transaction demand method might be used to distribute seigniorage on the basis of the long-run demand for money.

Reserve Centralization—Replacing the Existing Reserve Assets

International Clearing Union. As discussed earlier, the 1930s saw a breakdown in the international payments mechanism based on the gold standard's operation. A first shortcoming of this system related to liquidity. Although key currencies began to emerge as a source of liquidity during the first years of the twentieth century, gold production provided the major component of reserves. Since this component depended largely upon mining costs and the market gold price, gold as a source of liquidity could not always be assured to provide stable supplies. A second problem related to the rigidity of the adjustment mechanism under the gold standard. The 1930s experienced an asymmetrical adjustment mechanism whereby there was a deflationary bias; because surplus countries could more easily neutralize reserve gains and prevent inflationary internal adjustments than deficit countries could neutralize reserve losses and avoid deflation, the full burden of adjustment tended to fall on the deficit countries. A third problem concerned the disruptive influence that capital movements had on a country's payments balance. Capital flight associated with economic and political shocks largely resulted in the competitive devaluations of the 1930s. It was these problems that the 1943 Keynes plan for an International Clearing Union was attempting to solve.[6]

The purpose of the International Clearing Union was to extend to the international sphere the principles of domestic banking by establishing an international central bank. Rather than continuing the bilateral system of international payments of the 1930s, which was disruptive to any system of triangular trade, Keynes called for a system of multilateral clearing in which the International Clearing Union could be used primarily for the clearing and settlement of ultimate outstanding imbalances between central banks. This would help facilitate an efficient payments mechanism.

The operation of Keynes' plan required the creation of a new international currency, called bancor, that would replace the existing gold and key currency reserve assets. The value of each national currency and gold would be stated in terms of bancor. Deficit countries would have the option of setting imbalances either with gold or bancor, or both.

Since the cost of issuing bancor would virtually be zero, the International Clearing Union would have to distribute sizable amounts of seigniorage to its members. The proposed method was to distribute seigniorage in proportion to a country's average long-run demand for reserves—a transaction demand solution.

Keynes foresaw a declining role for gold in the international payments mechanism. The initial retention of gold as collateral for bancor was primarily designed to make his proposal more acceptable to conservative central bankers. Over time, Keynes hoped that gold's relative importance to bancor would decline, as well as its absolute significance. This would be accomplished by the International Clearing Union buying gold with bancor in unlimited quantities, but not selling gold.

A primary objective of the International Clearing Union was to modify the 1930s asymmetrical adjustment mechanism which promoted a deflationary bias. Keynes' method of putting pressure on both surplus and deficit countries to adjust included the following points. First, deficit and surplus countries would pay a penalty interest charge on their bancor deficits or deposits on a graduated scale after a stipulated proportion of their quotas had been reached. Second, deficit countries' automatic borrowing rights were restricted to 25 percent of their quotas in a given year; if their drawings exceeded 50 percent of their quotas, they could be forced by the International Clearing Union to provide gold collateral, adopt expenditure-switching devaluations, or have their borrowing privileges terminated. The intent of Keynes was not to rely upon automatic checks to balance accounts, but rather to provide a set of rules that would force both surplus and deficit countries to adjust.

Keynes' concept of international monetary reform was not warmly received in 1944, largely because of its revolutionary nature. But there are a number of arguments against his plan. First, one could not count on a steady growth of reserves from year to year, for there was no active policy of reserve creation on the part of the International Clearing Union; instead, reserves would increase according to member countries' average long-run demands. Also, doubts about a secular growth of reserves were raised, since although members' quotas would periodically be increased as foreign trade grew, member countries might not take advantage of such facilities.[7] A second major limitation concerns a potential inflationary bias of the International Clearing Union. Because gold would eventually be withdrawn from the payments mechanism, if financial discipline did not exist in bancor creation, surplus countries might experience large inflations as they accepted bancor payments from deficit nations.[8]

Triffin's XIMF. During the late 1950s, Robert Triffin formulated what would become known as "Triffin's Dilemma," which held that a basic problem of the dollar-gold system involved an inadequate liquidity mechanism. Because gold production did not provide adequate quantities of reserves during the 1950s, the need for reserve currencies, notably the U.S. dollar, arose. Because this required that the U.S. supply liquidity through its payment deficits, a confidence problem developed; doubts were raised about the U.S. ability to maintain asset convertibility and the value of the dollar. Maintaining confidence in the dollar required the U.S. to practice financial discipline and reverse its deficits; but in doing so it would restrict the growth of international liquidity in the form of reserve currencies—hence the dilemma.[9]

Unlike Keynes, who was basically concerned with improving the adjustment mechanism, Triffin primarily emphasized the liquidity problem of the dollar-gold system. His solution was to have countries initially maintain a portion of their gold and reserve currencies on deposit with an expanded International Monetary Fund (i.e., XIMF). In return they would receive bancor deposits which would be used in international transactions. Par values of national currencies and gold would be defined in terms of bancor. In the case of a "fundamental disequilibrium," a country could change its exchange rate. Eventually bancor would replace gold and reserve currencies as a means of settlement. Triffin advanced three reasons for this position. First, reserve currencies are vulnerable in their pledge to maintain asset convertibility into gold; thus their volume is subject to erratic changes. Second, the growth of international reserves should depend upon a stable expansion of bancor deposits, rather than upon random shifts in the reserve center's external deficits. Third, Triffin sympathized with foreign central bankers, notably the French, who objected to the U.S. having the unique privilege of obtaining seigniorage through its payment deficits.[10]

Because the XIMF would be earning interest on foreign exchange assets initially transferred to it, on bancor loans to deficit countries, and on bancor investments in member countries' capital markets, the seigniorage attributed to bancor deposits would be distributed to member countries. Triffin chose a market solution method of seigniorage distribution; by the XIMF paying interest on bancor deposits he felt they would be superior to gold as reserve assets.

The XIMF would provide a system of multilateral clearing and reserve creation for participating countries. Several methods would exist for creating reserves. First, reserves could be created by the XIMF granting loans to deficit countries; the initiative of liquidity expansion would come from the individual countries in this case. In this respect the Keynes and Triffin plans provided similar liquidity expansion facilities. A second method of creating reserves would be through the XIMF distributing reserves among its members by periodically granting bancor deposits to their accounts. Third, reserves could be created through XIMF open market operations. With the consent of the country in need of reserves, the XIMF could purchase its securities and government bonds with bancor, thus increasing its supply of liquidity. Triffin's plan therefore provided methods whereby the XIMF could take the initiative in creating reserves, unlike Keynes' plan which relied primarily upon the initiative of the borrowing countries.

Although the above discussion suggests that in the long run Triffin's plan could provide a greater potential for expanding reserves than Keynes' plan, it is not without limitations.[11] First, there is no real improvement in the adjustment mechanism, for there are no official pressures to force adjustments on debtor and creditor countries, except for the interest payments paid on bancor loans. Hence, there still may exist a devaluation bias in the adjustment mechanism. Second, there are some types of payment pressures that cannot necessarily be eliminated by increasing the supply of liquidity—for instance, a "fundamental disequilibrium" arising from political upheaval. Third, under a paper currency such as bancor, there is no guarantee that its purchasing power is assured. Triffin does not provide a means by which the holders of bancor would adequately be compensated in the event of inflation. Fourth, there is a potential problem involving the asset convertibility of bancor. Initially bancor deposits could be acquired by depositing gold or reserve currencies convertible into gold at the XIMF, subject to minimum acceptable levels. However, if the XIMF increased a country's bancor deposit through loans and/or open market purchases, so that it exceeded the minimum deposit requirement, the country could exercise its option to convert its excess bancor holdings into gold. Although Triffin's XIMF could make liquidity more flexible and responsive to world needs, it would face the familiar problems of asset convertibility and indequate adjustment incentives that plagued the dollar-gold standard.[12]

Reserve Centralization—Supplements to Existing Reserve Assets

Unlike the historic plans of Keynes and Triffin, which would have resulted in creating a new reserve asset that replaces the existing gold and key currency assets, a number of other proposals have been made to create new assets that would supplement the existing reserve assets. Among those which will be mentioned are the plans of Angell, Stamp, and Bernstein.

The Angell Plan. In 1961 James W. Angell stated that the primary defect of the dollar-gold system involved the contradiction of the role it assigned to gold. Angell contended that the supply of gold could not match its needs which included the role as an official reserve asset, a means of international settlement, and a medium of satisfying private speculators and hoarders. Yet the world clings to its role in the international payments system. He thus proposed to modify Triffin's treatment of gold, outlined above.

First, Angell opposed Triffin's allowing surplus countries to demand gold for part of their bancor holdings. He instead held that the XIMF could buy gold for bancor, but not sell gold for bancor. Because there would be only one-way asset convertibility, gold would be eliminated as a means of settling payment disequilibriums. Second, Angell favored Keynes' proposal of a system whereby both deficit and surplus nations would be encouraged to adjust and eliminate their external imbalances. He desired strong adjustment incentives similar to those of the Keynes plan—including the rights of the XIMF to impose graduated interest charges on deficit country liabilities, to demand that deficit nations undergo devaluation adjustments, to suspend interest payments on excess bancor holdings of surplus countries, etc. Although Angell's proposal might be more politically acceptable than Triffin's plan, in that it improves the treatment given to gold and the adjustment mechanism, it does not provide an adequate secular increase in reserves; Angell believed that over the long run there was no evidence that an increase in the volume of trade would require higher levels of reserves.[13]

The Stamp Plan. According to Maxwell Stamp, the fundamental shortcoming of the dollar-gold system was not the existence of a shortage of owned and borrowed reserves. Rather it rested on two propositions. First, there generally is an underutilization of resources among the advanced countries of the world. Second, the less developed countries normally require larger quantities of goods than are currently being produced. Stamp contended that in order to help facilitate and encourage increasing supplies of goods, a supplementary reserve asset should be created and distributed among the countries of the world for immediate spending.

Stamp emphasized that to be effective the credit facilities must be fully used; merely to increase borrowing privileges or quotas was not enough. Thus, he proposed that the seigniorage from the issue of a new international reserve asset under the IMF be distributed on an equitable basis to the less developed countries in the form of long-term developmental loans. These countries would spend these assets on the real goods and services produced in the developed countries, who by agreement would treat them as official reserves. The plan therefore served the dual purpose of increasing the supply of liquidity and providing developmental assistance to the less developed countries.[14]

There are several weaknesses in Stamp's plan. First, it presupposes that the advanced nations would be willing to convert real resources into the new paper assets created by the IMF. It also implies that developmental aid would be nonproject oriented. Political realities raise doubts that the advanced countries would allow the less developed countries to disproportionately benefit from the new reserve asset's seigniorage, or would permit developmental aid on a nonproject oriented basis. Second, since the certificates of deposit would be issued against long-term developmental loans, what is to guarantee their value? Doubts about their value arise when considering the ability of these countries to meet commitments on the principal and interest payments.

Bernstein's Composite Reserve Units. Another approach to increasing the quantity and flexibility of liquidity under the existing IMF arrangements comes from Edward M. Bernstein.[15] This approach, involving a new reserve asset called a composite reserve unit (i.e., CRU) has three basic features. First, the parities of all currencies would be fixed in terms of gold, and these parities would not be changed except after consulting with the IMF, presumably in the case of a "fundamental disequilibrium." Second, the role of gold as a medium of settlement would be continued, but only on the basis as a final reserve asset. Third, while retaining gold and reserve currencies as official reserves, a new reserve asset, CRU, would be created by the IMF.

The creation of CRU would require all major industrial nations to deposit stipulated amounts of their currencies with the IMF. In return the IMF would create against these deposits an equivalent amount of CRU over a number of years which would be used for two purposes. The CRU could be distributed to participating countries in proportion to their original contribution, and would serve as a medium of settlement. Initially, the deficit country would pay its creditors with reserve currencies, and a fixed proportion of gold and CRUs. As more CRUs were issued over time, the role of gold in settlements would decline. A second purpose would be for the IMF to loan CRUs to deficit countries; over time these countries would be expected to undergo equilibrating adjustments and pay back their borrowings from the IMF.

Although the CRU proposal provides promise for increasing the quantity and flexibility of reserves, it has a number of shortcomings. First, Bernstein's proposal does not improve the payments adjustment mechanism. Second, the basic problems of the dollar-gold system still exist, for the CRU is only a supplement to the existing assets; if the U.S. reversed its external deficit, a liquidity shortage could still arise. Third, if the creation of CRUs is limited to a certain amount per year, there is no reason to believe that quantity will be optimal since the liquidity needs of the world may not parallel this growth rate. Fourth, liquidity creation under the CRU proposal favors the industrially advanced nations, who would generally be more able to provide a gold guarantee for their currencies backing the CRU than the less developed countries.[16]

RESERVE CENTRALIZATION—AN SDR STANDARD

The use of SDRs as a reserve supplement under the dollar-gold system has been previously discussed. In 1969 the IMF adopted a new reserve asset, the SDR, which was to enhance the flexibility of international liquidity. This reserve supplement would be distributed to participating countries on the basis of existing IMF quotas—a demand-type method of seigniorage distribution—and pay to their holders an annual interest rate of 1.5 percent. Although SDRs have helped improve the flexibility of liquidity, the adjustment problems of the dollar-gold system were not eliminated: the U.S. could not unilaterally control its exchange rate with respect to other currencies; other nations did not generally have the incentive to make equilibrium changes in their exchange rates. A proposal of theoretical interest lies in the formation of a truly international currency by adopting an SDR standard.[17]

Under an SDR standard, all national currencies would be defined in terms of the SDR unit, the de jure numeraire. The other reserve asset, gold, would maintain a fixed and unchangeable exchange rate with the SDR; this would prevent any speculation over their conversion rate. Although SDRs would be the de jure numeraire, their success in contributing to an efficient payments system would depend upon the extent to which they could replace the dollar as the de facto international numeraire and intervention currency.

Making SDRs more attractive to use than dollars could be achieved in a number of ways. Central bankers would likely hold SDRs in preference to dollars, should the SDR interest rate be raised relative to that of dollar assets. Under the present arrangements, SDRs pay an annual interest rate of 5 percent on official net holdings, while dollar reserves can be held in interest-earning forms, such as government securities that provide substantially higher earnings. Another way of increasing the demand for SDRs would be to replace dollars with SDRs as the intervention currency in the foreign exchange markets. Having central banks hold working balances of SDRs rather than dollars could require the

IMF to declare that any public transactions in foreign exchange with a central bank must be solely in the domestic currency and SDRs. To illustrate, suppose the U.S. had an external deficit with Britain. The excess supply of dollars held by British commercial banks would be converted into SDRs at the Federal Reserve, which would then be taken back to the Bank of England for conversion into pounds.

For the U.S., an SDR standard would eliminate the Nth currency problem—that is, the U.S.'s inability to control its exchange rate with respect to other currencies, since other countries combined determine the international value of the dollar. An SDR currency that serves as both a de jure and de facto numeraire implies that the world would have N national currencies and an N + 1 international currency. The U.S. could unilaterally change its par value in terms of SDRs, for instead of the N-1 independently determined exchange rates of the dollar-gold standard, there are N independent exchange rates, where N equals the number of national currencies in the system. Diagram 6-1 illustrates a U.S. devaluation with respect to the SDR.

Diagram 6-1 is based upon the assumptions of Diagram 5-6 in the previous chapter. Suppose that the U.S./British exchange rate is initially established at point A. The price of the pound in terms of the dollar is denoted by the reciprocal of the slope of the ray OA (i.e., angle a). Now suppose that the U.S. legally devalued the dollar with respect to the SDR, shown by a drop in the SDR price of the dollar from OR to OS. *Ceteris paribus,* this would result in a depreciation of the dollar in terms of the pound; the dollar price of the pound would increase from the value of angle a to that of angle b.

Just because the SDR standard's elimination of the Nth currency problem implies that the U.S. exchange rate is not determined solely by the collective actions of all other countries combined, it does not follow that the U.S. has total control over its exchange rate. Because some countries have sizable trade relations with the U.S., a dollar depreciation against their currencies might leave them at a severe competitive disadvantage. In terms of the diagram, the pound, which is representative of the other currencies in the world, might be legally devalued along with and to the same extent as the dollar; the SDR price of the pound would fall from OQ to OT. No change in the dollar-pound exchange rate would occur, for it would be at its initial value (i.e., denoted by the value of angle a).

Besides enhancing the U.S.'s ability to devalue the dollar, it is argued that an SDR standard would aid other countries. Under the dollar-gold system, foreign governments protested about the asymmetry whereby the U.S. uniquely financed its deficits through dollar liabilities, while other governments' deficits had to be settled in reserve assets. It was generally felt that the U.S. should not have the advantage of exchanging its currency obligations for other countries' real resources. Under an SDR standard, the dollar would be treated as any other currency. U.S. dollars which accumulated in foreign central or commercial banks would be fully convertible into SDRs at the Federal Reserve. This asset convertibility means that U.S. deficits would also be financed through reserve assets.

Although an SDR standard might improve the adjustment mechanism and flexibility of reserves, the writers contend that such a system will not be part of any monetary agreement in the foreseeable future. Recent experience with the EEC's pursuit

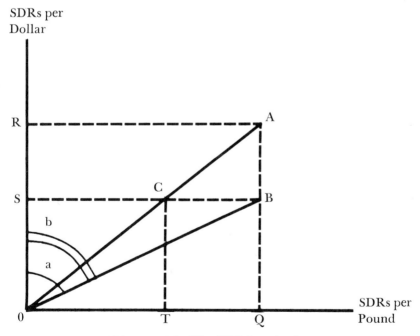

Diagram 6-1: The SDR Standard

of a single currency suggests that before a monetary union can exist there must be a political union. Given the current economic and political problems—energy shortages, high rates of global inflation, political turmoil among the EEC nations, etc.—it is doubtful whether there exists the degree of international cooperation essential for such an agreement. Another obstacle involves the disagreement over the distribution of SDRs among the advanced and less developed countries; the less developed countries often argue that the present SDR distribution formula, based upon participating countries' IMF quotas, should be modified so SDRs would be allocated disproportionately to the less developed countries as a means of developmental assistance. However, the industrially advanced countries, notably the U.S., have refused to accept this new approach. A last major limitation of adopting an SDR standard would be the transition problem of moving from the current system to one in which the SDR would become the international reserve, vehicle, and intervention currency. Making such a major monetary change could easily disrupt exchange market stability and confidence, thus resulting in a massive wave of destabilizing speculation.

THE RUEFF PLAN—INCREASING THE PRICE OF GOLD

In the 1960s and early 1970s the French economist Jacques Rueff wrote several papers suggesting that the fundamental problem of the dollar-gold system was not a shortage of reserves, but rather an excess stemming from an inadequate adjustment mechanism.[18] As Rueff pointed out, because the U.S. as a reserve center had the privilege of running payment deficits without losing official reserves, they did not have the effect of diminishing her money supply. The fact that there never was a contraction of aggregate demand in the U.S. corresponding to its deficits explained why those deficits continued. Another adverse consequence of the dollar-gold system was that there was a double pyramid of credit in the world. The dollars that went abroad as U.S. deficits were reinvested back in the U.S. by foreign central banks; but the same dollars, which supported the U.S. credit system, also supported expanding credit in foreign countries. As a result of this pyramid and the break in the link between the U.S. external and internal balance, Rueff contended that the dollar-gold standard's adjustment mechanism was inadequate.

Rueff's proposal involved an elimination of the dollar-gold system in order to improve the adjustment mechanism. His basic objective was to create a situation in which a deficit country would lose what a surplus country gains. This would provide a direct link between a country's internal and external balance, for its money supply would be tied to gold, hence nullifying the asymmetry where the reserve center uniquely benefits at the expense of the world through its currency liabilities.

The transition from the dollar-gold system to a gold standard would require the elimination of the reserve currencies (i.e., the dollar and sterling) from the payments system. To accomplish this, Rueff would have the U.S. and Britain buy back the largest part of their currency obligations with gold from foreign central banks. The problem was that both the U.S. and British gold stocks were insufficient to provide full asset convertibility. In 1967 Rueff proposed a once-and-for-all gold revaluation by about 200 percent, from $35 to $70 per ounce of gold. Although the increased gold price would increase the nominal value of existing gold assets, there would be no change in exchange rates among countries; in terms of Diagram 5-6, a U.S. and British devaluation with respect to gold of the same amount would result in a movement from some point, say Q, to another point closer to the origin (i.e., commensurate with the devaluation) on the initial ray, OQ. During the 1960s Rueff chose to double the price of gold, reflecting the rise in the world price level between 1934, when one ounce of gold equalled $35, and the late 1960s. By the early 1970s he modified his estimate and stated that higher world prices would require at least a tripling of the 1934 gold price. This was because the U.S. gold stock had fallen to about $11 billion, while its dollar liabilities to foreign public and private institutions combined surpassed $45 billion by the end of 1970. Since this threefold price increase would likely be inflationary, Rueff held that his proposal was no longer entirely adequate. However, a lesser gold revaluation could still aid the U.S. in paying back the most volatile portion of its dollar obligations.

Rueff contended that with the increased nominal gold reserves, the U.S. could pay off its dollar obligations without facing risks of inflation or deflation. This was because at the time of Rueff's proposal U.S. gold stocks equalled $13 billion, which approximately matched its outstanding dollar obligations to the world. A doubling in gold's price would increase U.S. gold reserves to $26 billion; the U.S. could use about half of its revalued reserves to repay foreign central bankers, thus retaining its initial cash position. Because Britain's gold reserves were insufficient to provide full asset convertibility at the revalued price, Rueff suggested that countries whose reserves would be increased in value by the gold revaluation make a long-term loan to Britain to enable it to liquidate its sterling obligations held by foreign central banks.

Rueff felt that international settlements in gold could be restored without any danger of insolvency, provided that gold's revaluation took place and the classical adjustment mechanism was adhered to. However, there are a number of objections to his plan. It is doubtful that deficit countries would be willing to accept deflationary adjustments in their internal balances. Also, the automatic nature of the classical adjustment mechanism is subject to question; based on the experience of the gold standard of the 1880–1914 period, there is little evidence showing that the "rules of the game" were obeyed. Furthermore, a doubling of gold's price might be inflationary since the suddenness with which reserves are increased could lead to excess liquidity immediately following the gold revaluation. Last, to encourage gold dishoarding, a once-and-for-all price change would have to convince speculators that gold would not again be revalued. If speculators felt that the revaluation would likely be repeated, gold hoarding might increase, thus imposing deflationary pressures and the possibility of a liquidity crisis.[19]

IMPROVING THE ADJUSTMENT MECHANISM— EXCHANGE RATE FLEXIBILITY

Floating Exchange Rates. Floating or flexible exchange rates refer to rates that are determined daily by the market forces of international supply and demand, without restrictions imposed by government policy on the extent to which rates can move.[20] Although there is no official exchange stabilization fund to defend a parity or a band around parity, the freedom of exchange rates to move in the market does not imply that they must significantly or erratically fluctuate; they will do so only if the underlying forces of supply and demand are unstable.

The relative advantages and disadvantages of floating exchange rates will next be discussed. However, an underlying thesis should first be pointed out: that while theoretical economists may embrace floating exchange rates for abstract reasons of overall economic efficiency, automaticity, etc., the practitioner (central banker) is not as interested in these dimensions as he is in having an institution available to him that provides liquidity. And this is provided under a system of fixed exchange rates. As will be pointed out, the concepts of liquidity and price-adjustment are antithetical in the sense that, given an efficient adjustment mechanism, floating exchange rates would require only minimal working-balance reserves.

The case for freely floating exchange rates is essentially the case for a free market economy in which there will be an efficient allocation of resources at least cost. According to Adam Smith, individuals seeking their own self interest and operating within the framework of a highly competitive market system would simultaneously, as though guided by an "invisible hand," promote the public interest by producing the goods and services wanted by society at maximum economic efficiency.[21] The argument for floating exchange rates rests upon the principle that a freely competitive market establishes a price that equates quantity supplied with quantity demanded, hence clearing the market. The diagram below illustrates the mechanics of automatic adjustment under a system of freely floating exchange rates.

Diagram 6-2 represents the foreign exchange market from the perspective of the U.S. Assuming that the supply-and-demand curves of West German marks initially intersect at point E, suppose the U.S. demand for Volkswagens increases, inducing a rise in the demand for marks from D_0 to D_1. Initially, there is a momentary tendency towards disequilibrium since the quantity demanded of marks exceeds the quantity supplied by Q_0-Q_2. As the U.S. consumers purchase marks to satisfy their demand for Volkswagens, the dollar depreciates by R_0-R_1, where a new equilibrium is reached at F. Now suppose that rising incomes induce West Germans to import more U.S. products. This would increase the supply of marks for the U.S. from S_0 towards S_1, resulting in a dollar appreciation towards the original exchange rate, R_0.

The case for floating exchange rates is summarized in the following arguments.[22] A first advantage of floating rates is their simplicity. Because the exchange rate is allowed to freely fluctuate according to international supply-and-demand forces, a mar-

116

ket equilibrium is established so that all excess and deficient quantities of any given currency are eliminated. Also, rather than having an exchange rate's movement being governed by formal rules of conduct for the participating countries, the floating system's simplified institutional arrangements imply that the exchange rate responds quickly to market forces. Therefore, the simplicity of floating rates implies that they may be relatively easy to enact and administer.

Another advantage stems from the continuous adjustment of market-determined rates. Because a floating rate is constantly adjusting to market forces, the adverse consequences of prolonged disequilibriums are eliminated. Because market equilibrium is

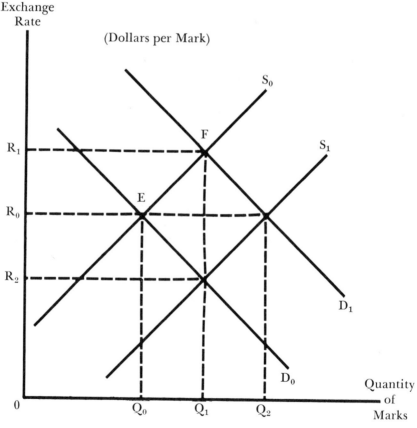

Diagram 6-2: Freely Floating Exchange Rates

attained there exists no need for governments to hold official foreign exchange reserves for exchange rate stabilization. Any holdings of national currencies would serve as working balances rather than for maintaining a certain exchange rate for a given country's currency.[23]

A third advantage of floating rates relates to their permitting countries more freedom to pursue their domestic policies than would occur under a system of pegged exchange rates. Assume one country faces a high rate of inflation relative to the rest of the world, thus inducing a deficit in its balance of payments. Because this would result in a depreciation of the inflating country's currency, the deficit would normally be reduced. Therefore, the reversing of an external deficit would not require the use of contractionary domestic policies which would disrupt a country's internal balance. Because the burden of balance-of-payments adjustment is borne by the exchange rate rather than domestic income adjustments, countries have more freedom to initiate policies promoting internal balance. Although domestic policies become relatively more independent under a system of floating rates, the desire of countries to avoid large, destabilizing exchange rate movements will limit the independence of countries pursuing their domestic goals.

But there also exist objections to a system of market determined rates.[24] A first argument contends that floating rates may become unstable, hence reducing the total volume of international transactions. This argument implies that an exogenous destabilizing force (i.e., a global energy shortage) might disrupt the exchange market to such a degree that the uncertainty and risk of wildly fluctuating international prices would discourage both lenders and borrowers from making long-term contracts. Although a lender could protect himself by insisting that a contract be written so that repayment of the loan would be in his own currency, this would merely burden the borrower with the uncertainty and risks of changing exchange rates. Therefore, should unstable exchange rates exist, not only would international cost and price comparisons be difficult to make, but the resulting uncertainty and risks tend to discourage foreign investments and capital flows among nations.

Another case against market-determined rates is based on the argument that floating rates will be destabilizing, so that even small exchange rate movements that result in uncertainty can elicit destabilizing speculative activity. This argument contends that a currency's depreciation will signal that the currency's international value will further decline in the future. Speculators will hence sell the currency, causing greater downward pressures on the exchange rate. The result is that speculators cause a larger currency depreciation than would normally exist. However, proponents of floating rates would counter-argue that speculative activity would actually be dampened rather than intensified. This is because speculators face the possibility that a depreciating/appreciating currency may become oversold/overbought and reverse its direction of movement in the exchange market.

Third, it is argued that should a country experience full employment with a high rate of inflation, a possibility exists that a currency depreciation will induce further upward pressures on domestic prices, thus resulting in the need for further depreciation. Assume a country has a balance of payments deficit that induces a depreciation of its exchange rate relative to those of other countries. Because this currency depreciation results in rising import prices, the deficit country would experience a rise in its price level; should the country's imports constitute a large part of its gross national product, rising import prices could considerably affect its cost of living. With the rise of inflation the deficit country's exports would become less competitive, thus inducing a further external deficit which results in another currency depreciation. The point is that should a depreciation induce higher inflation which results in a balance of payments deficit, this could set off another depreciation, higher inflation, and so forth. This suggests that a country with full employment and an external deficit may have to accept internal adjustments in the form of falling domestic spending (i.e., absorption) and income levels in order to reverse the imbalance.

A last argument against floating rates concerns their historical experience. From 1950–1962 Canada adopted a system of floating rates. It was the Canadian government's intention to utilize floating rates to maintain external balance, with monetary and fiscal policy free to concentrate on the objective of internal balance. This combination of policies worked remarkably well until the 1960–1962 period, when questionable stabilization policies were employed that resulted in a devaluation and pegging of the Canadian dollar.[25]

Although short-term capital movements generally behaved

in an orderly fashion, high Canadian interest rates induced destabilizing long-term capital inflows which continued to drive up Canada's exchange rate. By the late 1950s it was recognized that the premium on the Canadian dollar was inappropriate from a domestic stabilization viewpoint. In 1961 the Canadian monetary policy was eased considerably in order to lower the interest rate and increase aggregate spending. The initial effect of this policy was that the Canadian dollar began to float downward. However, by the end of 1961 confidence in the downward floating currency had weakened; this touched off a speculative run out of the dollar, this driving down the exchange rate further. On May 2, 1962, the Canadian dollar was pegged to the U.S. dollar at a rate of $1.00 U.S. = approximately $1.08 Canadian. This ingloriously ended Canada's experiment with a floating exchange rate.

The Canadian experience must be evaluated as inconclusive. Opponents of floating rates contend that the system resulted in dismal failure. However, defenders of market-determined rates hold that the problem was simply due to unsound domestic policies which induced a speculative attack against the Canadian dollar. The Canadian experience is not widely applicable for the defense of or case against floating exchange rates, for one cannot generalize from a case of one floating currency in a world of stable exchange rates to a world where all rates are market-determined.

Limited Exchange Rate Flexibility—Wider Bands. From World War II until December, 1971, members of the IMF agreed to maintain exchange rates not at a single point value but within plus/minus 1 percent around their declared parities. A country's exchange rate could remain flexible and respond to market forces so long as it remained within these limits. The monetary crises of the late 1960s and early 1970s led to the historic Smithsonian Agreements, at which the original bands were widened to plus/minus 2.25 percent around parity. However, by March, 1973, these Smithsonian bands no longer prevailed, for severe monetary crises induced Japan and Europe to initiate floating rates which resulted in movements outside the bands.

The band proposals date back to the days of the gold standard, where exchange rates were kept within small margins around par value due to the activities of profit motivated arbitragers.[26] These proposals attempt to take advantage of the favorable effects that stable exchange rates provide for international transactions and the flexible exchange rates' benefits of relieving governments of the need to use their domestic policy instruments in pursuit of external balance. The intended result of this compromise between fixed and flexible exchange rates is to ensure that market forces will be permitted to demonstrate the basic weakness or strength of a currency and prevent the foreign exchange market from degenerating into disorderly chaos.

As a result of the 1971 Smithsonian Agreements, the 2.25 percent bands around parity were designed to operate in the same manner as the 1 percent bands of Diagram 5-3 and Diagram 5-4. However, Diagram 3-2 suggests that one possible effect of increasing the degree of exchange rate flexibility would be to reduce the need for reserves. Although proponents of wider bands agreed that the Smithsonian bands were a step in the right direction, they would generally call for a much wider margin, say plus/minus 5 percent of the announced parity. Several possible advantages of adopting wider bands are outlined below.

A primary economic objective of the wider band is to enable central banks to penalize destabilizing speculation by those who believe that the official par value of a currency cannot be kept by its authorities. Under the dollar-gold system, speculators took advantage of its devaluation bias, for they essentially had a "one-way bet"—a chance to win with virtually no chance of losing. When speculators viewed a currency to be weak, by selling it they put additional downward pressure on the currency and increased its chance of being devalued. When changes in par values did occur, they generally were too infrequent and excessively large, hence rewarding speculators with substantial profits. Proponents of the wider band proposals contend that small and frequent parity changes would better penalize speculators than the large and delayed parity changes of the dollar-gold system. Because exchange rates could move according to market forces within a wide band, the chances for quick and large speculative profits are greatly reduced. Also, the "one-way bet" favoring speculation would be eliminated. For instance, as speculators continually sell a weak currency they must face the possibility that the currency has been oversold and will begin to appreciate. If losses become a reality, destabilizing speculation would likely be reduced.[27]

Second, although wider bands could not by themselves solve the rigidities and asymmetries of the dollar-gold standard's adjustment mechanism, their proponents contend that larger movements in market rates can help eliminate imbalances by setting in motion equilibrating movements of foreign trade and long-term capital. As a deficit country's exchange rate depreciates, its exports will become more competitive in the world while its imports become less competitive with domestic products, thus tending to reverse the trade imbalance. If the exchange rate change is considered to be permanent, the increase profitability of export and import-competing industries may induce new foreign investment in the country, or deter national investment abroad. In these ways, the payments balance may be improved.[28]

The original IMF bands and the subsequent Smithsonian bands were symmetrical in that the permissible appreciations or depreciations from parity were of the same magnitude. However, a case can be made for having a system of asymmetrical bands, notably in the form of a wider-upside band.[29] For instance, a monetary authority might allow its exchange rate to depreciate by 1 percent, but to appreciate by 5 percent from parity. Although there would still be a band 6 percent wide, its parity would not be in the center. Wider-upside bands would likely appeal only to a monetary authority that considers movements of its exchange rate around parity more likely to be in the direction of an appreciation than a depreciation. For example, West German central bankers traditionally would expect their under-valued mark to exhibit upward pressure in a free foreign exchange market. Wider-upside bands could help eliminate the dollar-gold system's depreciation bias, for the undervalued currencies would experience relatively larger appreciations than the overvalued currencies' depreciations.

Although wider margins may help alleviate small temporary disequilibriums and mitigate against destabilizing speculation, they cannot solve problems of extreme maladjustment. Among the limitations of wider bands are the following. First, any proposal designed solely to widen the band of movement around a fixed parity is inadequate, for it does not guarantee that the long-run equilibrium exchange rate will fall within the band. A substantial disequilibrium may require greater exchange rate adjustments than the band permits. Second, once the exchange rate of any country has reached the band's upper or lower limits, in effect it becomes a rigid, fixed rate that presents speculators with a "one-way bet." For example, at the band's lower limit and given continuing downward pressure, the market rate can depreciate only through devaluation; this would likely result in a wave of speculation. Third, a widened band would not alleviate the asymmetry of any payments mechanism in which one currency serves as an intervention currency and international numeraire. When there is a total band width of, say, 10 percent, the potential cross exchange rate spread between peripheral currencies is the full 10 percent. However, a reserve currency as the numeraire can differ from any peripheral currency by only 5 percent, or one-half the band's width. The reserve center's exchange rate would also continue to be determined by the collective actions of all other countries in the foreign exchange market.[30]

Limited Exchange Rate Flexibility—The Crawling Peg. The wider band proposals are intended to help improve the international adjustment mechanism and discourage destabilizing speculation. Because these proposals provide only once-and-for-all increases in the degree of freedom of market rates to adjust to changing circumstances, countries experiencing internal inflations or recessions might find their exchange rates approaching the outer limits of an inflexible band. Once this limit is reached, the country in effect would be back on a system of fixed exchange rates. Also, speculators would be provided with a "one-way bet" concerning the direction of future exchange rate changes through expenditure-switching policies.

In contrast with the dollar-gold system's adjustable pegged exchange rates, whereby exchange rate changes came about infrequently but suddenly, and usually in large amounts, and the wider band proposals which may in effect amount to a fixed exchange rate system in some cases, the crawling peg proposals suggest that a country should make small frequent changes in its currency's exchange rate, so that it creeps according to a pre-announced formula.[31] Both surplus and deficit countries would keep adjusting through expenditure-switching devaluations or revaluations until the ultimate desired exchange rate level was attained. Central banks would intervene in the foreign exchange markets to stabilize the rates as they crawled from level to level. Proponents of the crawling peg contend that it would offer the benefits of freely floating rates with the stability and predictability of fixed exchange rates. Several arguments are advanced to support this point.

First, a chief aim of the crawling peg is to reduce the adverse effects of speculative capital movements. When an exchange rate abruptly changes by, say, 10 percent, speculators that anticipate such an occurrence can make sizable profits. But as an exchange rate change within a given period becomes smaller, speculators also find their profit potential reduced. Suppose that a deficit country decides to devalue its currency at a rate of 2 percent annually under a crawling peg, and that the rest of the world's short-term interest rate is 6 percent. If she announces her crawling peg program, and simultaneously increases her interest rate to 8 percent, the motivation for speculators to move their funds outward is lost—the 2 percent capital loss due to the depreciation that speculators can avoid by investing their funds abroad for a year is just offset by the 2 percent they would forgo in higher domestic interest earnings. By offsetting the capital losses induced by a currency depreciation with higher interest earnings on domestic securities, a devaluing country can discourage speculative capital outflows.

Second, in providing additional exchange rate flexibility, a crawling peg would allegedly increase the effectiveness of monetary policy in achieving domestic goals in the short run.[32] According to Robert Mundell, under a system of fixed exchange rates monetary policy is frustrated in its domestic stabilization effects. Suppose Japan experiences inflation with external balance. To combat this internal disequilibrium, Japan's central bank sells government securities in the open market to lower its money supply and raise interest rates. This induces foreigners to invest in Japan, which increases its money supply and offsets the effect of the original restrictive monetary policy. Now suppose Japan adopts a crawling peg. In combating inflation, interest rates are again raised; this attracts foreign capital which puts upward pressure on the yen's exchange rate. However, in this case the yen appreciates; because this induces Japan's consumers to substitute imports for domestically produced goods, the original monetary contraction is reinforced. Therefore, a crawling peg would enhance the effectiveness of monetary policy in achieving domestic goals.[33] A criticism of Mundell's theory is that it can be meaningful only if the following assumptions are valid: (1) all capital flows are exclusively determined by interest rate differentials; (2) exchange rates are so rigidly fixed that there is no forward exchange premium or discount; (3) international capital is so flexible that the smallest interest rate differential sets flows in motion.[34]

Third, a crawling peg would supposedly prevent or inhibit

external imbalances induced by the following: gradual shifts in demand patterns arising from changes in incomes, etc.; gradual changes in international competitiveness or other supply factors which arise from changing labor or other resource costs; modest influences on trade balances due to changes in national tax and tariff policies. However, the crawling peg would not be conducive to combating large disturbances to external balance, such as wars or national disaster, that result in a "fundamental disequilibrium."[35]

Crawling peg proposals all share two common characteristics. They all impose a specified limitation on the maximum size of parity adjustments to be permitted in a fixed time period; for instance, parities could be automatically adjusted daily, weekly, or monthly in such a manner that the annual rate of change does not exceed 2 or 3 percent. They also link parity movements to objective economic criteria, notably reserve movements and market exchange rates. The proposals essentially differ in the degree of leeway left to national monetary authorities in determining parity movements; the possibilities range from a fully automatic scheme based on a rigid formula to one completely discretionary with preannounced changes in parities as part of economic policy.

A first automatic triggering mechanism is reserve flows. Target rates-of-reserve increases for each country would serve as a reference point in determining if a country's currency should be appreciated (depreciated) if its actual reserves exceeded (fell short of) their target. This suggests that world reserves would be broadly defined to include gold, reserve positions at the IMF, SDRs, and liquid assets in convertible foreign currencies.[36] However, using reserve changes as a triggering indicator does not necessarily reflect a true balance-of-payments position, for they can be induced by capital flows unrelated to underlying cost and price movements in a country.[37]

A second triggering mechanism would gear parity changes to actual movements in market (i.e., spot) exchange rates. The exchange parity at the beginning of any trading day would be equal to the average of market rates experienced during the previous year. Exchange parities would therefore be determined by a moving average of market rates. If the market rate was below the moving average, this would generally induce a depreciation of a currency, while a currency's appreciation would result from a market rate above the moving average. However, there are two major difficulties with this mechanism. First, market rates neglect the importance of nonmarket transactions, such as the purchase of marks for U.S. military forces in West Germany. Because these purchases exert no direct pressure on the market rate, the dollar could technically be weak even though it has a strong market position. Second, central bankers' interventions in the exchange market can influence the movement of a parity.

Besides having actual parity changes automatically linked to changes in the above objective triggering indicators, they could also be based upon discretionary economic policies that would use the objective indicators merely as guides; any devaluation/revaluation would depend solely upon the motivations of individual governments. But under any system of discretionary rules, there is the possibility that the system could freeze up and become rigid, thus resulting in less frequent parity changes than would be desirable. This is because governments are generally reluctant to bind themselves to courses of action that do not agree with their economic objectives. Also, competitive devaluations resulting in "beggar-thy-neighor" policies might result should countries attempt to maintain internal balance in times of global recession.

A variant of a totally discretionary mechanism would be one based upon presumptive rules. According to previous agreements, changes in automatic indicators such as market rates or reserve changes would signal for a change in exchange rates. Although a country would presumably be expected to undergo an exchange rate change as dictated by the objective indicator, the decision to make the change would be left to individual governments. However, failure officially to devalue or revalue a currency would necessitate an explanation to the IMF by the country involved. Any country that systematically ignored the presumptive rules and offered unacceptable justification would be open to economic sanctions (i.e., no credit from the IMF, duties imposed on its products by other countries, etc.).[38]

Although the crawling peg proposals attempt to make the adjustment mechanism more efficient and less prone to destabilizing speculation, several major limitations exist. First is the possible deterioration of financial discipline if governments can avoid adverse consequences of inflation through regular exchange rate depreciations. Second, unless a fully automatic triggering mechanism were adopted, a devaluation bias might exist because surplus countries could better forestall adjustments than deficit countries. Third, it is important whether parities are defined in terms of a reserve currency, gold, or some other numeraire. If a reserve currency served as the numeraire, the consequences of the Nth currency problem would again exist; the reserve center would not only lose control of its exchange rate, but a movement in its exchange rate with any other currency could be only half that of the cross rates between two nonreserve center countries.[39] Fourth, although a crawling peg might be successful for a small developing country that suffers from chronic inflation and who is heavily dependent upon international trade, it would likely be hard to apply to the industrialized reserve center nations whose currencies serve as a source of international liquidity.[40] As will later be discussed, the monetary crises of 1973–1974 raise doubts over whether such a system would be politically acceptable to the participating countries.

Limited Exchange Rate Flexibility—The Crawling Band. When comparing the wider band and crawling peg proposals, it is essential to realize that because they are intended to serve different functions they are complementary rather than competitive in their effects. A wider band mainly serves to discourage speculation and to reduce the need for reserves. It is not conducive to eliminating secular payments disequilibriums. Because a crawling peg would provide greater exchange rate flexibility over time, it would better serve to combat secular imbalances. Therefore, the wider band is often linked to the crawling peg—this is known as a crawling, or movable band.

Under a system of crawling bands, the market rate would float within a band, unhindered by the exchange rate operations of central bankers. However, once the band's intervention points were reached, the need for reserves would appear; deficit countries would experience reserve losses when defending the band's lower edge, while surplus countries would face the opposite. Because defending a disequilibrium rate over time could impose severe costs upon the countries concerned, a crawling band could be initiated. A politically determined triggering mechanism—probably reserve or market exchange rate changes—would indicate when the crawl should begin. Assuming an automatic, or a properly functioning discretionary or presumptive system, the devaluation/revaluation would then occur at a relatively slow rate of 2–3 percent annually. When the objective indicators showed that the imbalance was sufficiently reversed, the downward/upward crawl would cease; moderate exchange rate movements could again occur within the band.

Although the crawling band would not solve all the problems of the world's monetary system (i.e., liquidity and confidence), proponents contend that by improving the adjustment mechanism several advantages exist: a reduction in the need for reserves; a discouraging of speculation. The crawling band suffers from the same basic limitations of the crawling peg proposal. Of chief concern is the application of such a system to the industrially advanced, reserve center countries and its political acceptability by the participating countries.

The EEC's Joint Float.[41] A primary objective of the members of the European Economic Community (i.e., EEC) is to achieve monetary union. This suggests the necessity of attaining fixed parities between member currencies, and ultimately the adoption of a single money. In 1970 an EEC study group formulated the Werner Report, which called for the reduction and eventual elimination of exchange rate fluctuations among EEC currencies and complete liberalization of capital movements. Prior to the May and August, 1971, monetary crises, Community countries agreed to maintain a band whose maximum potential spread against the dollar's central rate was plus/minus 0.75 percent rather than the plus/minus 1 percent potential spread permitted under the IMF arrangements; this allowed EEC currencies to fluctuate 1.5 percent around par rate, suggesting a potential cross rate between EEC currencies of 3 percent. As previously discussed, between August and December of 1971 the world's currencies floated without band restrictions under the dollar standard. This ended with the Smithsonian Agreements which allowed currencies to fluctuate within plus/minus 2.25 percent of the dollar's spread of 4.5 percent around the par value, and a potential cross rate between EEC currencies of 9 percent. Similar to the cross parity example of the previous chapter, assume that the U.S. is the reserve center, while Britain and West Germany are peripheral countries: 1 mark = 100¢, and 1 pound = 200¢. With a band of plus/minus 2.25 percent around the par value, the following rates exist:

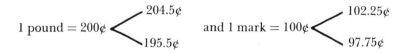

$$1 \text{ pound} = 200¢ \begin{cases} 204.5¢ \\ 195.5¢ \end{cases} \quad \text{and } 1 \text{ mark} = 100¢ \begin{cases} 102.25¢ \\ 97.75¢ \end{cases}$$

In terms of the mark, the pound could fluctuate within a range of 1 pound $=$ 2.09 marks (i.e., the pound's strongest position against the mark's weakest position—204.5¢/97.75¢) to 1 pound $=$ 1.91 marks (i.e., the pound's weakest position against the mark's strongest position—195.5¢/102.25¢). This is a range of 0.18 marks. Using the midpoint of the range, 2 marks, as a base, the cross rate between the mark and pound is 9 percent (i.e., 0.18/2).

Because the Smithsonian bands contradicted the Community's philosophy of a monetary union, in March, 1972, an agreement was made known to reduce the maximum potential cross rate between EEC currencies to 2.25 percent. This implied that the Community adopted a joint float, whose 2.25 percent band moved within the wider 4.5 percent Smithsonian band. The main feature of this system was that the exchange rate margins between EEC currencies would be narrowed while allowing Community currencies to float within the outer Smithsonian band with respect to the dollar. Full use of the Smithsonian band would be permitted for the Community. This arrangement became known as the "snake in the tunnel." The snake's maximum width represented the greatest possible exchange rate spread, vis-à-vis the dollar, between EEC currencies; the tunnel's maximum width signified the greatest allowable spread of Community exchange rates against the dollar as permitted by the Smithsonian Agreements.

Assuming that the EEC snake and Smithsonian tunnel are at their maximum widths, Diagram 6-3 illustrates the snake's movement within the tunnel over time. The maximum width of the tunnel, denoted by the outer band, R_1-R_2, is 4.5 percent. The snake's greatest potential width, denoted by R_3-R_4, is 2.25 percent (i.e., the maximum spread vis-à-vis the dollar between the weakest and strongest Community currencies). Note that the snake's width can be less than 2.25 percent in terms of the dollar, for the spread between the weakest and strongest Community currencies can become narrower or wider, depending on the strength of the demand for the individual currencies. It is also assumed that within the Community exchange rates can fluctuate according to market forces to the snake's outer limits before requiring EEC central bankers to intervene in the foreign exchange market with Community currencies, and that the EEC's inner band can move upward or downward (i.e., appreciate or depreciate) against the dollar by the full limits of the tunnel. In terms of the diagram, this implies that each EEC currency would also float with the Smithsonian band limits of R_1 and R_2. This is because a currency at different points in time could become both the strongest and the weakest currency within the Community.

The position of the snake is determined by market forces. The snake's position could change if market forces exerting pressure on any two Community currencies' exchange rates—that had moved in the opposite direction to the upper and lower limits of the snake—were of unequal magnitude. Suppose that the strongest and weakest currencies' exchange rates respectively moved to the upper and lower boundaries of the snake, and market forces pushing the strongest currency upward were of greater magnitude than those that pushed the weakest currency downward; then the Community snake would move toward the tunnel's upper edge, implying that EEC currencies as a group appreciated relative to the dollar. According to the Smithsonian Agreements, if the snake's position reached the tunnel's upper limit, EEC central bankers would purchase with the strongest Community currencies sufficient quantities of the excess dollars on the foreign exchange market to prevent the snake's movement out of the tunnel. Conversely, should market forces result in the EEC currencies depreciating relative to the dollar, so that the

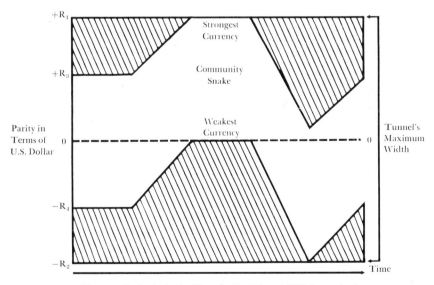

Diagram 6-3: Snake in the Tunnel—Quotation of EEC Currencies in Terms of the U. S. Dollar

snake fell to the tunnel's lower limit, Community central bankers would intervene in the foreign exchange market and purchase with dollars the excess quantities of weakest EEC currencies.

In addition to determining the snake's position within the outer Smithsonian tunnel, market forces also govern the width of the snake. According to the EEC formula, the maximum exchange rate spread (cross rate) between the strongest and weakest Community currencies vis-à-vis the dollar is 2.25 percent. However, within this constraint the snake could become narrower or wider, depending upon the market demand for individual Community currencies.

Diagram 6-4 makes the following assumptions. The maximum width of the Smithsonian tunnel is 4.5 percent in terms of the dollar, denoted by R_1-R_2. Also the maximum potential width of the Community snake with respect to the dollar is 2.25 percent, represented by R_3-R_4. Furthermore, market forces are assumed to initially result in the snake's actual width, denoted by ab, to be less than its potential width.

Suppose that during time period t_1-t_2 the strongest and weakest EEC currencies are both appreciating against the dollar, but the market demand for the strongest currency exceeds that of the weakest currency. In this case the former's rate of appreciation would be greater than that of the latter (i.e., the slope of

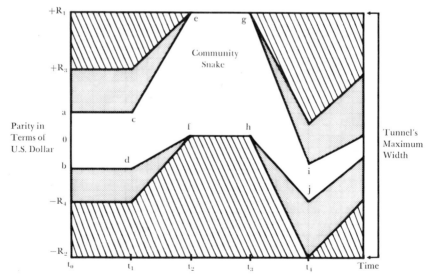

Diagram 6-4: Actual Width and Movement of the Snake in the Tunnel

ce exceeds that of df), so that at t_2 the snake's width would be ef, which is the maximum width of the snake (i.e., ef = 2.25 percent). Now suppose that during time period t_3-t_4 market forces result in the strongest and weakest Community currencies depreciating with respect to the dollar, but that the rate of depreciation of the strongest currency exceeds that of the weakest currency (i.e., gi is steeper than hj). The snake would gradually narrow; at t_4 the snake's width would be ij, where ij is less than gh.

From April, 1972, when the EEC's joint float within the Smithsonian band was formally adopted until the end of the year, the snake generally floated quite smoothly within the tunnel. However, by February, 1973, EEC currencies were sharply appreciating against the dollar due to the previously discussed international monetary crisis. On March 19, 1973, six Community members terminated the tunnel's existence, since the Smithsonian band could no longer be adequately defended through central bankers intervening in the foreign exchange market. Because EEC central bankers continued to maintain a maximum spread of 2.25 percent between their currencies, they kept the snake alive, but without a tunnel in which to float. After the March, 1973, crisis, the snake was turned into an unlimited joint float against the dollar; the world found itself with something new—a floating snake.

Throughout 1973 the Community countries were able to comply to their agreement to maintain exchange rates within the floating snake's boundaries. However, the Arab nations' decisions to restrict oil exports and increase oil prices resulted in significant inflationary pressures upon the economies of those countries that imported sizable quantities of oil. Particularly hurt were the Western European nations, who found their currencies weakening in the foreign exchange market as the energy crisis worsened. Due to a deteriorating 1973 payments balance and inflationary pressures induced by rising oil prices, in January, 1974, France chose to abandon its commitment to support the Community snake by floating the franc against all other currencies of the world. Not only did this result in France dropping out of the EEC's joint float against the U.S. dollar, but it reduced the EEC's chances of achieving monetary union and a single currency by 1980.

This chapter has discussed the advantages and disadvantages of several reforms of and alternatives to the dollar-gold system.

The first group of reforms related primarily to the problems of international liquidity and confidence; among these proposals were Keynes' International Clearing Union, Triffin's XIMF, the SDR standard, the Rueff plan, and the plans of Angell, Stamp, and Bernstein. The second group of reform proposals dealt primarily with improving the adjustment mechanism; these included freely floating exchange rates, the wider band proposals, the crawling peg, the crawling band, and the EEC's joint float. In light of these reform solutions, the next chapter will discuss the operation and success of the managed float, which has become the interim monetary mechanism from 1973–1976. It will be emphasized that since the international monetary system is based on political as well as economic dimensions, any lasting reform agreement will likely require much improved political and economic relations among participating countries.

CHAPTER 7

The Managed Float

INTRODUCTION

As discussed earlier, during the era of the dollar-gold system the IMF countries faced several adjustment problems that led to the system's breakdown. Among these were the following: first, there existed the probability that a deficit country (notably the United States) with a small involvement in international transactions could largely escape equilibrating internal and/or external adjustments. Second, since the United States as the reserve center did not lose reserves when financing an external deficit, it faced no significant pressure to undergo internal adjustments. A third problem was that because reserve losses were generally considered more critical than reserve gains, deficit countries faced greater pressure than surplus countries to undergo equilibrating exchange rate adjustments. This suggested an international adjustment mechanism with a devaluation bias. Fourth, the freedom of the United States to alter its exchange rate was limited. This was because it was generally held that a U.S. devaluation would create a destabilizing effect on other countries' internal balances sufficient to warrant their undergoing offsetting devaluations. Finally, most other deficit countries were reluctant to devalue their currencies, therefore admitting domestic financial irresponsibility to the world.

The above adjustment problems contributed to disequilibrium countries postponing internal and/or external adjustments as long as possible. During the last years of the dollar-gold system, exchange rate adjustments were undertaken by several IMF countries. But these adjustments generally were too late and too large. Also, because speculators were in effect able to anticipate a change in a currency's par value, they were able to make substantial profits from exchange rate realignments. This was demonstrated during the currency crises of 1971 and 1973. During the 1974 monetary crisis, the existing fixed exchange rate system became untenable. Temporary arrangements were made for the adoption of managed floating rates by the industrialized nations.

The industrialized world's 1973 movement to managed floating exchange rates was initially viewed to be an interim solution. Although the 1973 IMF meetings did consider reforming the international adjustment mechanism, no conclusion was reached regarding the future role of the managed float. The 1974 international monetary reform meetings never seriously considered reforming the adjustment mechanism. Because of the destabilizing effects of the oil crisis and the massive global inflation, it was recognized that a workable fixed exchange rate system was impossible. The financial community felt that a return to fixed exchange rates was unlikely until: (1) a new and realistic equilibrium was established among the major currencies; (2) the international monetary system could guarantee a more efficient adjustment mechanism, an improvement in the quality of reserves, and the avoidance of destabilizing capital flows. Because the managed float was behaving reasonably well, emphasis shifted from reform to evolution. Rather than focusing attention on how to reorganize the exchange rate mechanism, the question was how to make the managed float more operable. This point will be discussed later.

The purpose of this chapter is to analyze the nature of, need for, and effects of managed floating exchange rates. Their effects on global monetary stability, trade balances, and capital flows are of particular interest. In light of the problems confronting the world economy throughout the 1970s, an evaluation of the managed float's future role for the international monetary system will be made.[1]

THE MANAGED FLOAT: EXCHANGE MARKET ADJUSTMENTS

The basic purpose of a managed floating system is to establish a mechanism whereby exchange rates are managed by central bankers, rather than freely responding to international supply-and-demand forces. There currently exist two basic variants of this system—a two-tier exchange rate mechanism (dual exchange rates), and the practice of central bankers operating in the exchange markets in order to prevent short-term, disorderly movements in exchange rates (central-banker smoothing operations).

Two-Tier Exchange Rates.[2] As previously mentioned, a major problem of the dollar-gold system involved short-term, interest-sensitive, speculative capital flows which moved destructively across national borders. As seen during the international monetary crisis of 1973, these capital flows may result in national monetary authorities being unable to pursue independent monetary policies or defend pegged exchange rates. The primary objective of dual exchange rates is to prevent destabilizing speculative capital flows for current account (that is, commercial) transactions. This is accomplished in two ways. First, a floating exchange rate for financial transactions is established to insulate a country's external balance from net capital flow effects. Second, a pegged exchange rate is established for current account transactions. Although there has been no case where complete segregation of commercial and financial transactions has occurred, the dual exchange rate systems practiced by Belgium, France, and Italy during the 1970s have closely approximated this mechanism.

Under dual exchange rates a floating financial rate suggests that because the capital account remains in equilibrium, no "net" capital inflows to or outflows from a two-tier country can occur. This tends to insulate a country's external balance from capital flow effects. The following example illustrates this point. Assume a two-country model in which the United States and ROW (the rest of the world countries combined) operate in a dual rate system. Starting at equilibrium point E in Diagram 7-1, suppose the ROW demand for dollars increases from D_0 to D_1. This induces a ROW currency depreciation against the dollar of R_0-R_1. At R_1 each ROW currency unit buys fewer dollars (that is, each dollar buys more ROW currency units) than at R_0. This means that the profitability of U.S. investments in ROW has risen. United States investors therefore expand foreign investments, thus demrnding larger quantities of ROW currency. As United States investors purchase ROW currency, the ROW supply of dollars shifts from S_0 to S_1. At the same time, for ROW investors the lower exchange rate implies that foreign investments in the United States have become less profitable. As ROW foreign investments decline, fewer dollars are demanded. This is shown by the shift in the ROW demand for dollars from D_1 to D_2. All else being equal, the net effect of the United States demanding more ROW currency while the ROW demands fewer dollars is a reversal in the exchange rate's movement from R_1 to R_0. Financial market equilibrium is established at point G. In this manner a floating financial rate can promote capital account balance for a two-tier country.

Because dual exchange rates tend to insulate a balance of payments from net capital flow effects, any external imbalance would stem from current account disequilibria. However, pegged exchange rate systems (dollar-gold system) have the potential of becoming rigid. Under dual exchange rates a country facing a

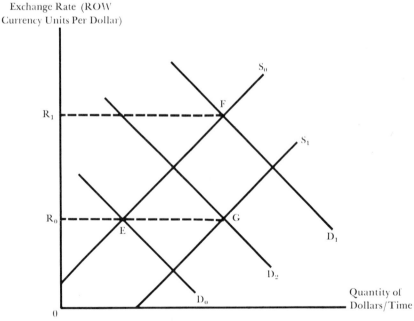

Diagram 7-1: *Financial Market Equilibrium under Dual Exchange Rates*

current account deficit might attempt to defend its commercial rate while at the same time prevent unacceptable decreases in its international reserve position. This could be accomplished through central bank interventions in both the commercial and financial markets. This is illustrated below.

In defending its commercial rate a deficit country could sell foreign currency (purchase its domestic currency) on the commercial market in sufficient quantities to restore equilibrium. This would result, however, in a deterioration of its reserve position. To replenish its lost reserves the two-tier country could enter the financial market and attempt to purchase with its currency equal quantities of foreign currencies. As Diagram 7-1 suggests, should a given country increase its demand for foreign currencies in the financial market, its exchange rate will depreciate. And this will induce increased net capital flows into that country.

Although a national monetary authority could attempt to intervene in the financial market in the above manner, its success depends on several factors. A deficit country that sold foreign currency on the commercial market would not want to purchase an equal amount of that currency on the financial market at a higher price. In order to avoid potentially large administrative costs in the form of capital losses, the deficit country would want the commercial rate at which it sold foreign currency to at least equal the financial rate at which it purchased foreign currency. Given the freely fluctuating rates of the financial market, this may not occur. Another factor is the extent to which a depreciation of the deficit country's financial exchange rate could induce net capital movements into the country. And this largely depends on the degree by which foreign investors are willing and able to substitute the investments of the deficit country for their domestic investments. Should foreign investors react adversely, the deficit country's financial rate depreciation might be unsuccessful in attracting the necessary amounts of foreign currency.

Although two-tier exchange rate systems have recently been used by Belgium, France, and Italy, there are factors that limit their ability to insulate a country's balance of payments from capital movements over a sustained period of time.[3] A primary limitation concerns the disruptive effect on capital movements that can occur when the commercial and financial rates split apart. For example, should a country face persistent external deficits, causing its financial rate to depreciate and diverge from its commercial rate, speculative intermarket transfers may result in a net capital movement out of the financial market. If speculators interpret this divergence to mean a further decline in the financial rate, they may continue selling the weakening currency. This would induce greater downward pressures on its financial rate and further disrupt the exchange market.

Another shortcoming of dual rates relates to their not providing adjustment incentives for disequilibrium countries. For example, it is likely that the very act of a deficit country's intervention in the financial market to replenish reserves lost when defending its disequilibrium commercial rate may not only postpone but also add to the magnitude of future commercial rate adjustments. Therefore, a two-tier mechanism facing prolonged, destabilizing market forces may evolve into a rigid system similar to the dollar-gold system. Although a two-tier mechanism may be beneficial in that it can provide a short-run insulation for a country's external balance against random and temporary monetary disturbances, dual rates should not be used for counteracting net capital movements caused by long-term, fundamental forces.

Central Bank Exchange Market Operations. A second type of managed float occurs when a central banker observing the country's currency floating downward or upward steps into the exchange market and purchases with other reserves its currency to prevent a depreciation or sells to prevent an appreciation. Because of the strong economic and political interdependence of national economies in today's shrinking world, a successful managed float requires the close cooperation and general acceptance by all concerned. However, this does not always exist. For example, immediately following the August, 1971, floating of the overvalued U.S. dollar, Japan's central bankers prevented market forces from establishing the dollar's true international value (that is "clean float"). They accomplished this by exchanging yen for dollars on the exchange market. But the United States did not agree to Japan's restricting the dollar depreciation. The United States viewed this as a "dirty float," whereby political disagreement over the dollar's rate resulted in Japanese central-banking operations modifying a free market solution.

As mentioned earlier, during the 1973 international monetary crisis it became apparent that the existing payments system was untenable. As a result the Smithsonian Agreements, which had provided that a freely fluctuating exchange rate could deviate by

2.25 percent from par value, were terminated. Temporary arrangements then went into effect for a managed float of the industrialized currencies. These informal arrangements recognized the need for support interventions by central bankers. But they were to occur only when smoothing operations were geared to the prevention of a "disorderly" exchange market and were acceptable to all concerned nations. The term disorderly was not defined, mainly to prevent speculators from anticipating the response of central bankers to a given exchange rate movement. The industrialized countries informally agreed that smoothing operations could be useful in overcoming the dangers of misguided speculation and the potential instability of reserve currencies. Under the managed float central bankers were to enter the exchange market only to reduce short-term fluctuations of an exchange rate induced by temporary destabilizing market forces or speculative attacks on currencies. At the same time they would permit that rate to adjust to changes in long-term international supply-and-demand forces. It was imperative that central bank cooperation would ensure that two countries did not simultaneously attempt to depreciate their currencies, one relative to the others. This could lead to competitive depreciations and other forms of beggar-thy-neighbor trade policies.

A managed float provides potential solutions to the adjustment problems that plagued the former dollar-gold system. These are essentially the previously discussed advantages of a freely floating exchange mechanism—simplified institutional arrangements, adjustment incentive and efficiency, continuous and symmetrical adjustments, and the like. Another advantage of managed floating is that it can permit adjustment to take place rapidly when there is a sudden change in underlying forces, such as the destabilizing effects of the Arab nations' decision to raise oil prices dramatically at the end of 1973. Under the dollar-gold system, the political and economic rigidities that governed the adjustment mechanism discouraged timely, equilibrating adjustments.

As previously mentioned, although the 1973–1974 IMF monetary reform meetings did not originally envision a managed floating system, several disruptive factors led to its recognition. First, most industrialized economies have experienced inflationary and deflationary forces, whose relative strengths are difficult to measure. Second, the 1970s global energy crisis has resulted in a transfer of purchasing power from the industrialized countries to oil exporting nations. As a result, there has been sizable disequilibria in the current accounts of industrialized countries. Third, serious supply shortages have developed, notably in basic materials. Fourth, international markets and capital movements have often militated against national economic policies. These rapid changes have left the industrialized countries with a high degree of uncertainty, which has made them reluctant to accept any binding international monetary reform agreement.

In view of the above events, the 1974 IMF meetings at Washington adopted the managed float as an interim system. However, they also established several guidelines that central bankers are to follow in maintaining an orderly exchange market and avoiding competitive exchange rate alterations.[4] Among these guidelines are the following: the prevention of erratic, week-to-week exchange-rate fluctuations; the practice of central bankers utilizing smoothing operations to moderate exchange rate movements from month-to-month and quarter-to-quarter; the maintenance of a confidential target zone of exchange-rate fluctuations within which a given rate should gravitate-within over the medium-term (that is, a period of about four years). This confidential zone is designed to reflect the underlying market forces affecting a given currency. But if it should become a disequilibrium zone over time, it could be redefined after the concerned nation consulted with the IMF. Therefore, unlike the dollar-gold system, the managed float encourages a disequilibrium country not to maintain an overvalued/undervalued exchange rate against sustained market pressure.

Problems of the Managed Float. As previously mentioned, the managed float was initially adopted by the major industrialized nations in response to the 1973 international monetary crisis. More formal rules were formulated at the 1974 IMF meetings in order to make the managed float a more operable system. By 1975 the managed float faced severe criticism from many members of the financial as well as academic community. Of particular concern was the ability of the managed float to maintain orderly exchange rates, to help governments establish more independent domestic economic policies, and to automatically equilibrate trade balances. These problems will next be discussed.

According to managed float proponents, a primary benefit of floating exchange rates derives from the greater freedom permitted economic policy in attaining domestic macroeconomic objectives. Given an efficient exchange rate adjustment mechanism domestic authorities could formulate economic policies without undue worries concerning the maintenance of a fixed parity, prolonged balance-of-payments disequilibria, destabilizing capital movements, and the like. However, the managed float has faced criticism concerning its limited ability in aiding countries to isolate their domestic economies from external forces. It has been contested that exchange rate movements transmit effects into the domestic economy, the result being no isolation. For example, assume that an appreciating currency reduces a country's exports, the result being a decline in its export industries. Facing this unpleasant circumstance, domestic policymakers must decide how to adjust their economy to the adverse effects induced by the exchange rate fluctuation.

A second source of controversy has involved the stability of exchange rate movements under the managed float. Because businessmen must have an environment of stable prices in order to make long-term commitments, exchange rate fluctuations are of paramount concern. What bothers businessmen involved in international transactions is that widely fluctuating exchange rates result in uncertainty and added risk to transactions. Sharp, unexpected currency movements can greatly reduce an anticipated profit margin in a very short time period. Businessmen can, however, protect themselves by hedging—that is, through purchases and sales of currencies in the foreign exchange markets. However, the greater the anticipated exchange rate fluctuations, the more costly hedging becomes. And given a greater transaction cost, the volume of international transaction and investment declines. Critics of the managed float point out that exchange rate movements during 1975 did not always gradually respond to long-term, fundamental economic forces. Rather than having their movements explained by the underlying value of a currency, exchange rate fluctuations were often triggered by political events, news headlines, etc. And this led to a disorderly exchange market.

Another area of controversy concerning the managed float has involved its adjustment efficiency—that is, its ability to automatically equilibrate trade balances. Among the current economic factors that may delay or offset the ability of floating rates to promote global adjustments are the following: the coincidence of cyclical upturns and downturns; the long lead-time between orders and deliveries of many products; the price-inelastic and persistent global demand for many high-technology goods; the tendency of the domestic demand for many imports to be primarily a function of disposable income rather than price changes.

Managed float critics point out that the 1970s experience has indicated a lack of correlation between exchange rate fluctuations and trade balance movements.[5] It is argued that a currency depreciation at best has only a temporary effect on the trade balance. Therefore, movements in exchange rates do not solve fundamental problems that underlie a currency's value. The reason for this is that changes in currency values do not affect the relative price of products, which depends on real factors. This is because currencies are essentially yardsticks by which relative prices are measured. For example, regardless of the value of the dollar relative to the mark, a pound of copper mined in the United States still will trade for the same given amount of West German beer. What occurs instead is that the yardsticks readjust via changes in nominal prices of copper and beer in the currencies. In other words, the nominal prices will change to maintain equal real prices.

Based on the above argument, two conclusions follow. First, a nation cannot improve its trade balance through currency depreciation. No competitive advantage will be achieved, since nominal prices will change but real prices remain constant. Second, a country that finds its currency depreciating in the exchange market will suffer from an above-average inflation rate. Given a currency depreciation, if real prices remain constant the country's nominal prices must rise faster than those of other countries.

Summary and Conclusions

The economic and political events of the post–World War II era have often had a disruptive influence on the international payments mechanism. The dollar-gold system broke down in 1971 in response to the severe wave of speculative capital movements that resulted from a loss of confidence in the existing fixed exchange rate system. Although the return to fixed parities under the Smithsonian Agreements brought temporary order to the payments mechanism, the 1973 international monetary crisis resulted in its termination. It was then recognized that a workable fixed exchange rate mechanism required a much more stable environment than that which existed in 1973—thus the industrialized countries' adoption of the managed float. As pointed out, the efficiency of the managed float has been a controversial issue. Not only must the managed float face the previously discussed criticism involving trade balance equilibrating efficiency, exchange rate stability, and the independence of domestic economies, but it also faces problems of successfully operating during times of changing economic and political relationships among countries.

A primary area of concern for the managed float is the recent problem faced by the industrialized nations—how to finance their oil imports from OPEC. Since the industrialized world will likely face continued oil-induced, trade account deficits with OPEC, the question is how these imbalances can be sustained. Historically, the remedy would imply the use of official reserves until a given country's external deficit reached "fundamental disequilibrium" proportion. Currency devaluation, internal deflation, and import restrictions would then be possible adjustment alternatives. Under the current managed float mechanism, currency depreciation would be called for. However, these remedies are limited in the current situation. Rather than eliminating their deficit with the OPEC nations, these remedies tend to result only in shifting the adjustment burden among the industrialized countries. This is because OPEC nations will not be able to employ productively all of the enormous increases in oil revenues that they will be receiving in the next few years. Therefore, it is unrealistic to think that the above adjustment policies can substantially reduce the large OPEC surpluses. A real test for the managed float arises over whether deficit countries will have sufficient discipline to refrain from the use of beggar-thy-neighbor trade policies which proved so harmful in the 1930s.

In order to help the oil-importing countries finance their oil bills, it has generally been argued that the OPEC surplus dollars should be recycled to deficit nations, mainly through the Euro-currency market. However, this creates capital flow problems for the managed float. First is the funnel effect on the entire Euro-currency market—money is being drawn from all sectors of the market, but is being returned to just a few banks. The IMF does have its oil facility, designed to help needy countries that cannot attract sufficient capital inflows to finance their oil imports. But a coordinated effort among all concerned must be made to prevent rates from diverging unduly from a pattern considered to be conducive to the achievement of global equilibrium. Second, to the extent the OPEC nations place the bulk of their dollars in short-term investments, there exists the danger of switches among currencies. This suggests that such volatile short-term capital flows may not always produce a result consistent with medium-term equilibrium. Therefore, the managed float will have to include special measures—including overseas borrowing by government agencies and exchange market intervention through the use of reserves—to guard against destabilizing market forces.

This chapter has provided an analysis of the nature, operation, and problems of managed floating exchange rates. Although there exist questions concerning the managed float's stability and adjustment efficiency, the evidence is not yet conclusive concerning its overall merits. Throughout 1975 much of the academic and financial community was leaning toward the return to fixed exchange rates. However, this is not likely to take place until a more stable international economic order is achieved.

Notes

CHAPTER 2

1. See Valéry Giscard d'Estaing, "The International Monetary Order," in *Monetary Problems of the International Economy*, ed. R. Mundell and A. Swoboda (Chicago: University of Chicago Press, 1969), pp. 7–19.
2. Tibor Scitovsky, *Requirements of an International Reserve System*, Essays in International Finance, no. 49 (Princeton: International Finance Section, Princeton University, 1965).
3. M. Clement, R. Pfister, and K. Rothwell, *Theoretical Issues in International Economics* (Boston: Houghton Mifflin Co., 1967), p. 214.
4. Maurice Parsons, "Stabilizing the Present International Payments System," *The International Adjustment Mechanism* (Federal Reserve Bank of Boston, 1969), p. 41.
5. See Benjamin J. Cohen, *Adjustment Costs and the Distribution of New Reserves*, Studies in International Finance, no. 18 (Princeton: International Finance Section, Princeton University, 1966), pp. 3–5.
6. Clement, Pfister, and Rothwell, *Theoretical Issues in International Economics*, pp. 216–218.
7. Ibid., pp. 218–220.
8. See Cohen, *Adjustment Costs and the Distribution of New Reserves*, pp. 5–11.
9. Ibid., pp. 22–92.
10. Robert A. Mundell, *Monetary Theory* (Pacific Palisades, Calif.: Goodyear Publishing Co., 1971), pp. 137–141.
11. Thomas E. Davis, "The Problem of Confidence in International Reserve Assets," *Monthly Review* (Federal Reserve Bank of Kansas City, August/September, 1968), p. 8.

12. The short-run confidence problem is also discussed as the "crisis problem." See Robert A. Mundell, *International Economics* (New York: Macmillan Company, 1968), pp. 282–287.
13. Davis, "The Problem of Confidence in International Reserve Assets," p. 6.
14. Ibid.
15. This model is adapted from Harry Johnson, "Theoretical Problems of the International Monetary System," in *International Finance*, ed. R. N. Cooper (Baltimore: Penguin Books, 1969), pp. 323–327.
16. This analysis is largely adapted from Richard N. Cooper, "The Relevance of International Liquidity to Developed Countries," *American Economic Review* 58, (May, 1968): 626–629.
17. Ibid., p. 629.
18. Richard N. Cooper, *The Economics of Interdependence* (New York: Council on Foreign Relations, 1968), pp. 21–27.

CHAPTER 3

1. See Fritz Machlup, *International Payments, Debts, and Gold* (New York: Scribner's, 1964), chaps. 10–13. See also John Williamson "International Liquidity: A Survey," *Economic Journal* 83 (September, 1973): 685–746.
2. International Monetary Fund, *International Financial Statistics* (Washington, September, 1973), p. 17.
3. Ibid.
4. Ibid., p. 36.
5. See Eberhard Reinhardt, "The Role of Key Currencies," in *Convertibility - Multilateralism - Freedom*, ed. W. Schmitz (New York:

Springer Publishing Co., 1972), pp. 275–283.
6. See Gottfried Haberler, *Prospects for the Dollar Standard*, reprint no. 3 (Washington: American Enterprise Institute, 1972, pp. 9–10.
7. This example is adapted from Richard Ward, *International Finance* (Englewood Cliffs, N. J.: Prentice-Hall, Inc., 1965), p. 183.
8. International Monetary Fund, *Annual Report* (Washington: 1963), p. 16.
9. David S. Cutler, "The Operations and Transactions of the Special Drawing Account," *Finance and Development* (December, 1971), pp. 18–23.
10. J. J. Polak, "Some Reflections on the Nature of Special Drawing Rights," *IMF Pamphlet Series*, no. 16 (1971), p. 5. See also D. S. Cutler and D. Gupta, "SDRs: Valuation and Interest Rate," *Finance and Development* 11 (December, 1974): 18–21; D. Gupta, "The First Four Years of SDRs," *Finance and Development* 11 (June, 1974): 6–9, 31.
11. Cutler and Gupta, "SDRs: Valuation and Interest Rate," pp. 18–21.
12. Philip Rushing, "The Reciprocal Currency Arrangements," *New England Economic Review* (November-December, 1972), pp. 3–15.
13. "Swaps: Tool to Promote Orderly Exchange Markets Again in Use," *IMF Survey* (December 17, 1973), pp. 365–366.
14. Diagram 3-1 is adapted from Richard E. Caves and Ronald W. Jones, *World Trade and Payments: An Introduction* (Boston: Little Brown and Co., 1973), p. 416. Copyright © 1973

by Little, Brown and Company, Inc.). Reprinted by permission.

15. For a discussion of the interdependence of economic policies among countries, see Cooper, *The Economics of Interdependence,* chap. 6.

16. See J. M. Flemming, *Towards Assessing the Need for International Reserves,* Essays in International Finance, no. 58 (Princeton: International Finance Section, Princeton University, 1967), pp. 3–4.

17. This model is adapted from Herbert G. Grubel, *The International Monetary System* (Baltimore: Penguin Books, 1969), pp. 34–39.

18. Ibid., pp. 31–34.

19. Ibid., chap. 3.

20. See Clement, Pfister, and Rothwell, *Theoretical Issues in International Economics,* pp. 410–436.

21. See Fritz Machlup, *The Need for Monetary Reserves,* Princeton Reprints in International Finance, no. 5 (Princeton: International Finance Section, Princeton University, 1966); B. J. Cohen, *Balance of Payments Policy* (Baltimore: Penguin Books, 1969), chap. 3.

22. See M. J. Flanders, *The Demand for International Reserves,* Studies in International Finance, no. 27 (Princeton: International Finance Section, Princeton University, 1971).

23. Clement, Pfister, and Rothwell, *Theoretical Issues in International Economics,* p. 428.

24. H. R. Heller, "Optimal International Reserves," *Economic Journal* 76 (June, 1966): 301.

25. See Herbert G. Grubel, "The Demand for International Reserves: A Critical Review of the Literature," *Journal of Eco-nomic Literature* 9 (December, 1971): 1148–1166.

26. The problem of how to achieve a target level of reserves in a world of stable exchange rates is discussed in Cooper, "The Relevance of International Liquidity to Developed Countries," pp. 625–636.

27. Heller, "Optimal International Reserves," pp. 296–311. See also W. Sellekaerts and B. Sellekaerts, "Balance of Payments Deficits, the Adjustment Cost, and the Optimum Level of International Reserves," *Welwirtschaftliches Archiv,* vol. 109, pt. 1 (1973), pp. 1–17; P. B. Clark, "Optimum International Reserves and the Speed of Adjustment," *Journal of Political Economy* 78 (March/ April, 1970): 356–376.

28. Robert Clower and Richard Lipsey, "The Present State of International Liquidity," *American Economic Review, Papers and Proceedings* 58 (May, 1968): 594–595.

29. T. Balogh, "International Reserves and Liquidity," *Economic Journal* 70 (June, 1960): 363–364.

30. See J. F. Flemming, "International Liquidity: Ends and Means," *IMF Staff Papers* 8 (December, 1961): 439–463. See also Flemming, *Toward Assessing the Need for International Reserves,* pp. 5–11.

31. These indicators are found in the following sources: International Monetary Fund, *Annual Report* (Washington: 1969), pp. 17–28, 424, 448; Walter S. Salant, *Practical Techniques for Assessing the Need for Reserves,* reprint no. 198 (Washington: Brookings Institution, 1971), pp. 284–285.

32. International Monetary Fund, *Annual Report* (Washington: 1969), pp. 26–28.
33. Salant, *Practical Techniques for Assessing the Need for Reserves*, p. 282.
34. Quantitative projections of reserve needs are found in P. B. Kenen and E. B. Yudin, "The Demand for International Reserves," *Review of Economics and Statistics* 47 (August, 1965): 242-250. See also H. R. Heller, "The Transaction Demand for International Means of Pay ments," *Journal of Political Economy* 76 (January/February, 1968): 141–145.

CHAPTER 4

1. See W. E. Beach, *British International Gold Movements and Banking Policy, 1881–1913* (Cambridge, Mass.: Harvard University Press, 1935); W. A. Brown, Jr., *The Gold Standard Reinterpreted, 1914–1934* (New York: National Bureau of Economic Research, 1934).
2. This analysis is based on that found in Lester V. Chandler, *The Economics of Money and Banking* (New York: Harper and Row, 1973), pp. 20–23.
3. Diagrams 4-5 and 4-6 are reproduced with permission from Charles P. Kindleberger, *International Economics* (5th ed.; Homewood, Ill.: Richard D. Irwin, Inc., 1973 c.).
4. Delbert A. Snider, *Introduction to International Economics* (Homewood, Ill.: Richard D. Irwin, 1971), pp. 330–333.
5. David Hume, "Of the Balance of Trade," in *International Finance*, ed. R. N. Cooper (Balti-

more: Penguin Books, 1969), pp. 25–37.
6. Snider, *Introduction to International Economics*, p. 334.
7. For a more complete discussion of the income-specie-flow mechanism, see Ingo Walter, *International Economics* (New York: Ronald Press Co., 1968), pp. 325–332.
8. Diagram 4-7 is adapted from Mundell, *International Economics*, pp. 217–222. See also A. C. Day and S. T. Beza, *Money and Income* (New York: Oxford University Press, 1960), pp. 550–553.
9. Day and Beza, *Money and Income*, pp. 553–554.
10. Kindleberger, *International Economics*, p. 262.
11. See Mundell, *International Economics*, pp. 222–227.
12. Robert Triffin, "The Myths and Realities of the So-Called Gold Standard," in *International Finance*, ed. R. N. Cooper (Baltimore: Penguin Books, 1969), p. 46.
13. For a discussion of the historical conditions during the gold standard era, see Day and Beza, *Money and Income*, pp. 555–557; J. H. Jones, "The Gold Standard," *Economic Journal* 43 (December, 1933): 563–565; C. H. Walker, "The Working of the Pre-War Gold Standard," *Review of Economic Studies* 1-2 (1933–1935): 196–209.
14. Triffin, "The Myths and Realities of the So-Called Gold Standard," p. 51.
15. C. O. Hardy, *Is There Enough Gold?* (Washington: Brookings Institution, 1936), p. 42.
16. Triffin, "The Myths and Realities of the So-Called Gold Standard," p. 51.

17. A. Maddison, "Growth and Fluctuations in the World Economy," *Banca Nazionale del Lavoro Quarterly Review* (June, 1962), pp. 189–190.

18. Triffin, "The Myths and Realities of the So-Called Gold Standard," p. 41.

19. Arthur I. Bloomfield, *Monetary Policy Under the Gold Standard: 1880–1914* (Federal Reserve Bank of New York, 1959), pp. 25–26, 52–55. See also Richard S. Sayers, *Bank of England Operations, 1890–1914* (London: P. S. King and Son, 1936).

20. Bloomfield, *Monetary Policy*, pp. 55–56.

21. Ibid., p. 50.

22. See J. A. Stovel, *Canada in the World Economy* (Cambridge, Mass.: Harvard University Press, 1959), p. 60.

23. Arthur I. Bloomfield, *Short-Term Capital Movements Under the Pre-1914 Gold Standard*, Studies in International Finance, no. 11 (Princeton: International Finance Section, Princeton University, 1963), pp. 44–45.

24. Ibid.

25. Ibid., pp. 83–89. See also M. Simon, "The Hot-Money Movement and the Private Exchange Pool Proposal of 1896," *Journal of Economic History* 20 (March, 1960): 31–50.

26. Peter H. Lindert, *Key Currencies and Gold: 1900–1913*, Studies in International Finance, no. 24 (Princeton: International Finance Section, Princeton University, 1969), pp. 1–2.

27. Ibid., pp. 25–26.

28. Michael A. Heilperin, "The Case for Going Back to Gold," in *World Monetary Reform*, ed. H. G. Grubel (Stanford, Calif.: Stanford University Press, 1963), p. 334.

29. Grubel, *The International Monetary System*, p. 132.

CHAPTER 5

1. Council of Economic Advisers, *Annual Report* (Washington: January, 1964), pp. 134–148.

2. Snider, *Introduction to International Economics*, pp. 347–348.

3. Grubel, *The International Monetary System*, pp. 132–134.

4. Diagram 5-1 and this discussion are adapted from Michael W. Keran, "An Appropriate International Currency—Gold, Dollars, or SDRs?," *Review* (Federal Reserve Bank of St. Louis, August, 1972), p. 10.

5. The discussion and model are adapted from Grubel, *The International Monetary System*, pp. 128–131.

6. Copyright © 1971 by Harcourt Brace Jovanovich, Inc., and reprinted with their permission from *International Economics*, by Mordechai E. Kreinin. See also Haberler, *Prospects for the Dollar Standard*, pp. 11–12.

7. See Robert A. Mundell, "The International Disequilibrium System," *Kyklos* 14 (1961): 154–172.

8. For a discussion of the asymmetries of the dollar-gold system, see Peter B. Kenen, "The Costs and Benefits of the Dollar as a Reserve Currency—Convertibility and Consolidation," *American Economic Review, Papers and Proceedings* 63 (May, 1973): 191–193.

9. See L. B. Yeager, *International Monetary Relations* (New York: Harper and Row, 1966), pp. 99–104.

10. For a discussion of the benefits

and costs of being a reserve center, see Herbert G. Grubel, "The Benefits and Costs of Being the World Banker," *National Banking Review* 2 (December, 1964): 189–212. See also Robert Z. Aliber, "The Benefits and Costs of Being the World Banker—A Comment," *National Banking Review* 2 (March, 1965): 409–410.

11. Keran, "An Appropriate International Currency—Gold, Dollars, or SDRs?," pp. 10–11.

12. See Mundell, *International Economics,* pp. 195–198.

13. See R. N. Cooper, "Eurodollars, Reserve Dollars, and Asymmetries in the International Monetary System," *Journal of International Economics* 2 (September, 1972): 325–345; J. Williamson, *The Choice of a Pivot for Parities,* Essays in International Finance, no. 90 (Princeton: International Finance Section, Princeton University, 1971).

14. Diagram 5-6 is based upon Mundell, *Monetary Theory,* pp. 115–119.

15. The discussion and Diagram 5-7 are adapted from A. C. Day, "Institutional Constraints and the International Monetary System," in *Monetary Problems of the International Economy,* ed. R. Mundell and A. Swoboda (Chicago: University of Chicago Press, 1969), pp. 333–342.

16. The discussion is based on R. Carbaugh and L. S. Fan, "Policy Considerations in International Monetary Crises," *Rivista Internazionale di Scienze Economiche e Commerciali* 21 (October, 1974): 955–967.

17. This diagram is adapted from Day, "Institutional Constraints

and the International Monetary System," pp. 334–336.

18. This implies that under a system of pegged exchange rates, fiscal policy is relatively better suited for internal balance operations than monetary policy. See Robert A. Mundell, "The Appropriate Use of Monetary and Fiscal Policy under Fixed Exchange Rates," *IMF Staff Papers* 9 March, 1962): 70–77. See also Caves and Jones, *World Trade and Payments,* pp. 371–376; Dernburg, Thomas F., and McDougal, Duncan M., *Macroeconomics* (New York: McGraw-Hill, 1972), pp. 292–297.

19. E. W. Clendenning, *The Euro-Dollar Market* (London: Oxford University Press, 1970), p. 1.

20. Milton Friedman, "The Euro-Dollar Market: Some First Principles," *Review* (Federal Reserve Bank of St. Louis, July, 1971), pp. 17–18.

21. This example is adapted from Robert Z. Aliber, *The International Money Game* (New York: Basic Books, 1973), pp. 99–100.

22. Clendenning, *The Euro-Dollar Maket,* p. 151.

23. Harry Johnson, *Further Essays in Monetary Economics* (Cambridge, Mass.: Harvard University Press, 1973), pp. 353–358.

24. Keran, "An Appropriate International Currency—Gold, Dollars, or SDRs?," pp. 10–12.

25. "Dollar Devaluation Takes Effect," *IMF Survey* (February 26, 1973), pp. 49–51.

26. "Questions About the Dollar," *Economic Report* (New York: Manufacturers Hanover Trust Co., June, 1973).

27. *Survey of Current Business* (January, 1974), p. 5-2.

28. Stephen P. Magee, "Currency

Contracts, Pass-Through, and Devaluation," in *Brookings Papers on Economic Activity,* ed. A. M. Okun and G. L. Perry (Washington: Brookings Institution, 1973), pp. 305–309.

29. H. B. Junz and R. R. Rhomberg, "Price Competitiveness in Export Trade Among Industrial Countries," *American Economic Review, Papers and Proceedings* 63 (May, 1973): 412–418.

CHAPTER 6

1. Robert Z. Aliber, "Gresham's Law, Asset Preferences, and the Demand for International Reserves," *Quarterly Journal of Economics* 81 (November, 1967): 628–638.
2. J. M. Culbertson, "Alternative International Monetary Systems," *Recent Changes in Monetary Policy and Balance of Payments Problems,* Hearings Before the Committee on Banking and Currency, 88th Congress, First Session (Washington: Government Printing Offices, 1963), pp. 331–344.
3. See Benjamin J. Cohen, "The Seigniorage Gain of an International Currency: An Empirical Test," *Quarterly Journal of Economics* 85 (August, 1971): 495–496. See also Ronald I. McKinnon, *Private and Official International Money: The Case for the Dollar,* Essays in International Finance, no. 74 (Princeton: International Finance Section, Princeton University, 1969), pp. 17–23; Fritz Machlup, "The Cloakroom Rule of International Reserves: Reserve Creation and Resources Transfer," *Quarterly Journal of Economics* 79 (August, 1965): 337–355.

4. Cohen, "The Seigniorage Gain of an International Currency: An Empirical Test," p. 494.
5. Herbert G. Grubel, "The Distribution of Seigniorage from International Liquidity Creation," in *Monetary Problems of the International Economy,* ed. R. Mundell and A. Swoboda (Chicago: University of Chicago Press, 1969), pp. 275–280. See also Grubel, *The International Monetary System,* pp. 156–166.
6. John Maynard Keynes, "Proposals for an International Clearing Union," in *World Monetary Reform,* ed. Herbert G. Grubel (Stanford, Calif.: Stanford University Press, 1963), pp. 55–79.
7. Fritz Machlup, *Plans for Reform of the International Monetary System,* Special Papers in International Finance, no. 3 (Princeton: International Finance Section, Princeton University, 1962), pp. 28–30.
8. For an evaluation of the advantages and disadvantages of Keynes' plan, see Robert Triffin, *Gold and the Dollar Crisis* (New Haven: Yale University Press, 1960), pp. 90–102. See also Robert Triffin, *Europe and the Money Muddle* (New Haven: Yale University Press, 1962), pp. 93–109; Friedrich A. Lutz, *The Keynes and White Papers,* Essays in International Finance, no. 1 (Princeton: International Finance Section, Princeton University, 1943).
9. For a discussion of "Triffin's Dilemma" and the expanded International Monetary Fund, see Triffin, *Gold and the Dollar Crisis,* chap. 7.
10. See Robert Triffin, "The Coexistence of Three Types of Reserve Assets," *Banca Nazionale*

del Lavoro Quarterly Review (June, 1967), pp. 107–134.

11. Machlup, *Plans for Reform of the International Monetary System*, pp. 32–33.

12. See L. B. Yeager, "The Triffin Plan: Diagnosis, Remedy, and Alternatives," *Kylos* 14 (1961): 285–312; James Angell, "The Reorganization of the International Monetary System: An Alternative Approach," *Economic Journal* 71 (December, 1961): 691–708.

13. See Angell, "The Reorganization of the International Monetary System: An Alternative Proposal," pp. 691–708.

14. See Maxwell Stamp, "The Stamp Plan—1962 Version," in *World Monetary Reform*, ed. H. G. Grubel (Stanford, Calif.: Stanford University Press, 1963), pp. 80–89.

15. See Edward M. Bernstein, "The Further Evolution of the International Monetary System," *Moorgate and Wall Street* (Summer, 1965). See also his paper "The Bernstein Approach," in *Monetary Reform and the Price of Gold*, ed. Randall Hinshaw (Baltimore: Johns Hopkins Press, 1967), pp. 53–73.

16. These limitations of Bernstein's CRU proposal are adapted from Walter, *International Economics*, pp. 455–456. For a summary of an alternate CRU proposal, see J. D. Dewey, "The Evolving International Mechanism: The Report of the Group of Ten," *American Economic Review* 55 (May, 1965): 53–73.

17. This discussion is based upon Keran, "An Appropriate International Currency—Gold, Dollars, or SDRs?," pp. 15–19.

18. See Jacques Rueff's following papers: "The West is Risking a Credit Collapse," *Fortune* (July, 1961), pp. 126–127, 262–268; "The Rueff Approach," in *Monetary Reform and the Price of Gold*, ed. Randall Hinshaw (Baltimore: Johns Hopkins Press, 1967), pp. 37–46; "They Used to Call Me Cassandra," in *Convertibility, Multilateralism, and Freedom*, ed. W. Schmitz (New York: Springer Publishing Co., 1972), pp. 75–82.

19. For a discussion of the effects of reducing the price of gold, see Fritz Machlup, "Comments on the 'Balance of Payments,' and a Proposal to Reduce the Price of Gold," *Journal of Finance* 16 (1961): 186–193.

20. This discussion is based upon Milton Friedman's classic essay "The Case for Flexible Exchange Rates," in *Readings in International Economics*, ed. Richard E. Caves and Harry G. Johnson (Homewood, Ill.: Richard D. Irwin, 1968), pp. 413–437. See also Harry G. Johnson, "The Case for Flexible Exchange Rates, 1969," *Review* (Federal Reserve Bank of St. Louis, June, 1969), pp. 12–23; James E. Meade, "The Case for Variable Exchange Rates," *Three Banks Review* (September, 1955), pp. 3–27.

21. Adam Smith, *The Wealth of Nations* (New York: Modern Library, originally published in 1776), p. 423.

22. The case for and against floating rates is summarized in Clement, Pfister, and Rothwell, *Theoretical Issues in International Economics*, pp. 258–272.

23. See Egon Sohmen, *Flexible Exchange Rates* (Chicago: Univer-

sity of Chicago Press, 1961), pp. 71–72.

24. See Charles P. Kindleberger, "The Case for Fixed Exchange Rates, 1969," *The International Adjustment Mechanism* (Federal Reserve Bank of Boston, 1969), pp. 93–108.

25. See A. F. Plumptre, *Exchange-Rate Policy: Experience with Canada's Floating Rate,* Essays in International Finance, no. 81 (Princeton: International Finance Section, Princeton University, 1970). See also James E. Pesando and Lawrence B. Smith, "Monetary Policy in Canada," in *Monetary Policy in Twelve Industrial Countries,* ed. Karel Holbik (Federal Reserve Bank of Boston, 1973), pp. 85–88.

26. For a discussion of the bank proposal, see George N. Halm, *The Band Proposal: The Limits of Permissible Exchange Rate Variations,* Special Papers in International Finance, no. 6 (Princeton: International Finance Section, Princeton University, 1965). See also William Fellner, "On Limited Exchange-Rate Flexibility," in *International Finance,* ed. R. N. Cooper (Baltimore: Penguin Books, 1969), pp. 212–227.

27. Lawrence B. Krause, *Fixed, Flexible, and Gliding Exchange Rates,* reprint no. 205 (Washington: Brookings Institution, 1971), pp. 333–334.

28. Cooper, *The Economics of Interdependence,* p. 229. See also C. M. Van Vlierden, "Some Implications of Flexible Exchange Rates, Including Effects on Forward Markets and Transitional problems," in *Approach to Greater Flexibility of Exchange Rates,* ed. George Halm (Prince-

ton: Princeton University Press, 1970), pp. 277–279.

29. A wider-upside band would contain a bias favoring a currency's appreciation, while the opposite holds for a wider-downside band. See George H. Chittenden, "Asymmetrical Widening of the Bands Around Parity," in *Approaches to Greater Flexibility of Exchange Rates,* ed. George Halm (Princeton: Princeton University Press, 1970), pp. 245–249. See also George Halm, "Widening the Band for Permissible Exchange Rate Fluctuations," *The International Adjustment Mechanism* (Federal Reserve Bank of Boston, 1969), pp. 121–134.

30. See Leland B. Yeager, "A Skeptical View of the 'Band' Proposal," *National Banking Review* 4 (March, 1967): 291–297. See also Giuliano Pelli, "Why I Am Not in Favor of Greater Flexibility of Exchange Rates," in *Approaches to Greater Flexibility of Exchange Rates,* ed. George Halm (Princeton: Princeton University Press, 1970), pp. 202–208.

31. See James E. Meade, "The International Monetary Mechanism," *Three Banks Review* (September, 1964), pp. 3–25. See also John H. Williamson, *The Crawling Peg,* Essays in International Finance, no. 50 (Princeton: International Finance Section, Princeton University, 1965). James Meade credits the original idea of the crawling peg to J. Black. See J. Black, "A Proposal for the Reform of Exchange Rates," *Economic Journal* 76 (1966): 288–295.

32. George W. McKenzie, "International Monetary Reform and the

Crawling Peg," *Review* (Federal Reserve Bank of St. Louis, February, 1969), pp. 15–23.

33. This analysis is based upon Robert A. Mundell, "Capital Mobility and Stabilization Policy Under Fixed and Flexible Exchange Rates," *Canadian Journal of Political Science* 29 (November, 1963): 475–485.

34. See J. H. Furth, "International Monetary Reform and the Crawling Peg," *Review* (Federal Reserve Bank of St. Louis, July, 1969), pp. 21–25.

35. Richard N. Cooper, "Flexing the International Monetary System: The Case for Gliding Parities," *The International Adjustment Mechanism* (Federal Reserve Bank of Boston, 1969), p. 147. See also Richard N. Cooper, "Sliding Parities: A Proposal for Presumptive Rules," in *Approaches to Greater Flexibility of Exchange Rates,* ed. George Halm (Princeton: Princeton University Press, 1970), pp. 251–259.

36. Cooper, "Flexing the International Monetary System: The Case for Gliding Parities," pp. 150–151.

37. See J. M. Blin and F. H. Murphy, "The Smoothed Exchange Rate Approach to Parity Adjustment," discussion paper no. 39, The Center for Mathematical Studies in Economics and Management Science (Evanston, Ill.: Northwestern University, March, 1973), pp. 8–9.

38. Cooper, "Sliding Parities: A Proposal for Presumptive Rules," p. 251.

39. See Krause, "Fixed, Flexible, and Gliding Exchange Rates," pp. 334–337. See also Edward Howle and Carlos Moore, "Rich-ard Cooper's Sliding Parities: A Proposed Modification," *Journal of International Economics* 1 (1971): 429–436; John Williamson, *The Choice of a Pivot for Parities,* Essays in International Finance, no. 90 (Princeton: International Finance Section, Princeton University, 1971).

40. For a discussion of Brazil's experience with the crawling peg, see "The 'Crawling Peg' Works in Brazil," *Business Week* (September 16, 1972), pp. 56–64.

41. This discussion is adapted from the following papers: Günter Wittich and Masaki Shiratori, "The Snake in the Tunnel," *Finance and Development* (June, 1973), pp. 9–13, 38; Marie H. Lambert and Patrick B. de Fontenay, "Implications of Proposals for Narrowing the Margins of Exchange Rate Fluctuation Between the EEC Currencies," *IMF Staff Papers* 18 (1971): pp. 646–664; Giogio Basevi, "When the Snake Gets Out of the Tunnel," *Metroeconomica* 24 (September/December, 1972): 245–253.

CHAPTER 7

1. The material in this chapter is largely adapted from Robert J. Carbaugh, "The Controlled Float: Exchange Market Adjustments," *Nebraska Journal of Economics and Business* (Summer, 1975), pp. 53–63.

2. For an in-depth study of dual exchange rates, see Phillip Rushing, "The Two-Tier Exchange Rate System," *New England Economic Review* (Federal Reserve Bank of Boston, March-April, 1974), pp. 13–27. See also J. M. Flemming, "Dual Exchange Rates for Current and Capital

Transactions: A Theoretical Examination," in *Essays in International Economics* (Cambridge, Mass.: Harvard University Press, 1971), chap. 12.

3. Rushing, "The Two-Tier Exchange-Rate System," pp. 18–27.

4. "Guidelines for Management of Floating to be Used by Board in Consultations," *IMF Survey* (June 17, 1974), pp. 181–183.

5. See "The Drift Back to Fixed Exchange Rates," *Business Week* (June 2, 1975), pp. 60–63.

Selected Bibliography

BOOKS

Beach, W. E. *British International Gold Movements and Banking Policy, 1881–1913.* Cambridge, Mass: Harvard University Press, 1935.

Bernstein, Edward M. "The Bernstein Approach." In *Monetary Reform and the Price of Gold,* edited by Randall Hinshaw, pp. 53–73. Baltimore: Johns Hopkins Press, 1967.

Bloomfield, Arthur I. *Monetary Policy Under the Gold Standard: 1880–1914.* Federal Reserve Bank of New York, 1959.

Brown, W. A., Jr. *The Gold Standard Reinterpreted, 1914–1934.* New York: National Bureau of Economic Research, 1934.

Caves, Richard E., and Jones, Ronald W. *World Trade and Payments.* Boston: Little, Brown and Co., 1973.

Chandler, Lester V. *The Economics of Money and Banking.* New York: Harper and Row, 1973.

Chittenden, George H. "Asymmetrical Widening of the Bands Around Parity." In *Approaches to Greater Flexibility of Exchange Rates,* edited by George Halm, pp. 245–249. Princeton: Princeton University Press, 1970.

Clement, M., Pfister, R., and Rothwell, K. *Theoretical Issues in International Economics.* Boston: Houghton Mifflin Co., 1967.

Cohen, B. J. *Balance of Payments Policy.* Baltimore: Penguin Books, 1969.

Cooper, Richard N. *The Economics of Interdependence.* New York: Council on Foreign Relations, 1968.

Cooper, Richard N. "Flexing the International Monetary System: the Case for Gliding Parities." In *The International Adjustment Mechanism,* pp. 141–156.

Federal Reserve Bank of Boston, 1969.

Cooper, Richard N. "Sliding Parities: A Proposal for Presumptive Rules." In *Approaches to Greater Flexibility of Exchange Rates,* edited by George Halm, pp. 251–259. Princeton: Princeton University Press, 1970.

Day, A. C. "Institutional Constraints and the International Monetary System." In *Monetary Problems of the International Economy,* edited by R. Mundell and A. Swoboda, pp. 333–342. Chicago: University of Chicago Press, 1969.

Day, A. C., and Beza, S. T. *Money and Income.* New York: Oxford University Press, 1960.

Fellner, William. "On Limited Exchange-Rate Flexibility." In *International Finance,* edited by Richard N. Cooper, pp. 212–227. Baltimore: Penguin Books, 1969.

Friedman, Milton. "The Case for Flexible Exchange Rates." In *Readings in International Economics,* edited by Richard E. Caves and Harry Johnson, pp. 413–437. Homewood, Ill.: Richard D. Irwin, 1968.

Giscard d'Estaing, Valéry. "The International Monetary Order." In *Monetary Problems of the International Economy,* edited by R. Mundell and A. Swoboda, pp. 7–19. Chicago: University of Chicago Press, 1969.

Grubel, Herbert G. "The Distribution of Seigniorage from International Liquidity Creation." In *Monetary Problems of International Economy,* edited by R. Mundell and A. Swoboda, pp. 269–282. Chicago: University of Chicago Press, 1969.

Grubel, Herbert G. *The International Monetary System.* Baltimore: Penguin Books, 1969.

Hardy, C. O. *Is There Enough Gold?* Washington: Brookings Institution, 1936.

Heilperin, Michael A. "The Case for Going Back to Gold." In *World Monetary Reform,* edited by H. G. Grubel, pp. 329–342. Stanford, Calif.: Stanford University Press, 1963.

Hume, David. "Of the Balance of Trade." In *International Finance,* edited by Richard N. Cooper, pp. 25–37. Baltimore: Penguin Books, 1969.

Johnson, Harry. "Theoretical Problems of the International Monetary System." In *International Finance,* edited by R. N. Cooper, pp. 303–334. Baltimore: Penguin Books, 1969.

Johnson, Harry. *Further Essays in Monetary Economics.* Cambridge, Mass.: Harvard University Press, 1973.

Keynes, John Maynard. "Proposals for an International Clearing Union." In *World Monetary Reform,* edited by Herbert G. Grubel, pp. 55–79. Stanford, Calif.: Stanford University Press, 1963.

Kindleberger, Charles P. *International Economics.* Homewood, Ill.: Richard D. Irwin, 1968.

Kreinin, Mordechai E. *International Economics.* New York: Harcourt Brace Jovanovich, 1971.

Machlup, Fritz. *International Payments, Debts, and Gold.* New York: Scribner's, 1964.

Magee, Stephen P. "Currency Contracts, Pass-Through, and Devaluation." In *Brookings Papers on Economic Activity,* edited by A. M. Okun and G. L. Perry. Washington: Brookings Institution, 1973.

Mundell, Robert A. *International Economics.* New York: Macmillan, 1968.

Mundell, Robert A. *Monetary Theory.* Pacific Palisades, Calif.: Goodyear Publishing Co., 1971.

Parsons, Maurice. "Stabilizing the Present International Payments System." In *The International Adjustment Mechanism,* pp. 41–52. Federal Reserve Bank of Boston, 1969.

Reinhardt, Eberhard. "The Role of Key Currencies." In *Convertibility-Multilateralism-Freedom,* edited by W. Schmitz, pp. 275–283. New York: Springer Publishing Co., 1972.

Rueff, Jacques. "The Rueff Approach." In *Monetary Reform and the Price of Gold,* edited by Randall Hinshaw, pp. 37–46. Baltimore: Johns Hopkins University Press, 1967.

Rueff, Jacques. "They Used to Call Me Cassandra." In *Convertibility-Multilateralism-Freedom,* edited by W. Schmitz, pp. 75–82. New York: Springer Publishing Co., 1972.

Sayers, Richard S. *Bank of England Operations, 1890–1914.* London: P. S. King and Son, 1936.

Snider, Delbert A. *Introduction to International Economics.* Homewood, Ill.: Richard D. Irwin, 1971.

Stamp, Maxwell. "The Stamp Plan—1962 Version." In *World Monetary Reform,* edited by Herbert G. Grubel, pp. 80–89. Stanford, Calif.: Stanford University Press, 1963.

Stovel, J. A. *Canada in the World Economy.* Cambridge, Mass.: Harvard University Press, 1959.

Triffin, Robert. *Gold and the Dollar Crisis.* New Haven: Yale University Press, 1960.

Triffin, Robert. *Europe and the Money Muddle.* New Haven: Yale University Press, 1962.

Triffin, Robert. "The Myths and Realities of the So-Called Gold Standard." In *International Finance,* edited by Richard N. Cooper, pp. 38–61. Baltimore: Penguin Books, 1969.

Walter, Ingo. *International Economics.* New York: Ronald Press, 1968.

Ward, Richard. *International Finance.* Englewood Cliffs, N. J.: Prentice-Hall, 1965.

Yeager, Leland B. *International Monetary Relations.* New York: Harper and Row, 1966.

ARTICLES AND PERIODICALS

Aliber, Robert Z. "The Benefits and Costs of Being the World Banker—A Comment." *National Banking Review* 2 (March, 1965): 409–410.

Aliber, Robert Z. "Gresham's Law, Asset Preferences, and the Demand for International Reserves." *Quarterly Journal of Economics* 81 (November, 1967): 628–638.

Angell, James. "The Reorganization of the International Monetary System: An Alternative Approach." *Economic Journal* 71 (December, 1961): 691–708.

Balogh, T. "International Reserves and Liquidity." *Economic Journal* 70 (June, 1960): 357–377.

Basevi, Giorgio. "When the Snake Gets Out of the Tunnel." *Metroeconomica* 24 (September/December, 1972): 245–253.

Bernstein, Edward M. "The Further Evolution of the International Monetary System." *Moorgate and Wall Street,* Summer, 1965.

Carbaugh, R. J., and Fan, L. S. "Policy Considerations in International Monetary Crises." *Rivista Internazionale di Scienze Economiche e Commerciali* 21 (October, 1974): 955–967.

Carbaugh, R. J. "The Controlled Float: Exchange Market Adjustments." *Nebraska Journal of Economics and Business,* Summer, 1975, pp. 53–63.

Clark, P. B. "Optimum International Reserves and the Speed of Adjustment." *Journal of Political Economy* 78 (March/April, 1970): 356–376.

Clower, Robert, and Lipsey, Richard. "The Present State of International Liquidity." *American Economic Review, Papers and Proceedings* 58 (May, 1968): 586–595.

Cohen, Benjamin J. "The Seigniorage Gain of an International Currency: An Empirical Test." *Quarterly Journal of Economics* 85 (August, 1971): 494–507.

Cooper, Richard N. "The Relevance of International Liquidity to Developed Countries." *American Economic Review* 58 (May, 1968): 625–636.

Cooper, Richard N. "Eurodollars, Reserve Dollars, and Asymmetries in the International Monetary System." *Journal of International Economics* 2 (September, 1972): 325–345.

Cutler, David S. "The Operations and Transactions of the Special Drawing Account." *Finance and Development,* December, 1971, pp. 18–23.

Davis, Thomas E. "The Problem of Confidence in International Reserve Assets." *Monthly Review* (Federal Reserve Bank of Kansas City), August/September, 1968, pp. 3–12.

Dewey, J. D. "The Evolving International Mechanism: the Report of the Group of Ten." *American Economic Review* 55 (May, 1965): 53–73.

"Dollar Devaluation Takes Effect." *IMF Survey,* February 26, 1973, pp. 49–51.

"First Outline of Reform to Governors." *IMF Survey, Annual Meetings Issue Supplement,* October 8, 1973, pp. 305–308.

Flemming, J. F. "International Liquidity: Ends and Means." *IMF Staff Papers* 8 (December, 1961): 439–463.

Grubel, Herbert G. "The Benefits and Costs of Being the World Banker." *National Banking Review* 8 (December, 1964): 189–212.

Grubel, Herbert G. "The Demand for International Reserves: A Critical Review of the Literature." *Journal of Economic Literature* 9 (December, 1971): 1148–1166.

Heller, H. R. "Optimum International Reserves." *Economic Journal* 76 (June, 1966): 296–311.

Heller, H. R. "The Transactions Demand for International Means of Payments." *Journal of Political Economy* 76 (January/February, 1968): 141–145.

Howle, Edward, and Moore, Carlos. "Richard Cooper's Gliding Parities: A Proposed Modification." *Journal of International Economics* 1 (November, 1971): 429–436.

Johnson, Harry. "The Case for Flexible Exchange Rates, 1969." *Review* (Federal Reserve Bank of St. Louis), June, 1969, pp. 12–23.

Jones, J. H. "The Gold Standard." *Economic Journal* 43 (December, 1933), 551–574.

Junz, H. B., and Rhomberg, R. R.

"Price Competitiveness in Export Trade Among Industrial Countries." *American Economic Review, Papers and Proceedings* 63 (May, 1973): 412–418.

Kenen, Peter B. "The Costs and Benefits of the Dollar as a Reserve Currency—Convertibility and Consolidation." *American Economic Review, Papers and Proceedings* 63 (May, 1973): 189–198.

Kenen, Peter B., and Yudin, E. B. "The Demand for International Reserves." *Review of Economics and Statistics* 47 (August, 1965): 242–250.

Keran, Michael W. "An Appropriate International Currency—Gold, Dollars, or SDRs?" *Review* (Federal Reserve Bank of St. Louis), August, 1972), pp. 8–19.

Lambert, Marie H., and de Fontenay, Patrick B. "Implications of Proposals for Narrowing the Margins of Exchange Rate Fluctuations Between the EEC Currencies." *IMF Staff Papers* 18 (November, 1971): 646–664.

Machlup, Fritz. "The Cloakroom Rule of International Reserves: Reserve Creation and Resources Transfer." *Quarterly Journal of Economics* 79 (August, 1965): 337–355.

McKenzie, George W. "International Monetary Reform and the Crawling Peg." *Review* (Federal Reserve Bank of St. Louis), February, 1969: pp. 15–23.

Meade, James E. "The Case for Variable Exchange Rates." *Three Banks Review*, September, 1955, pp. 3–27.

Meade, James E. "The International Monetary Mechanism." *Three Banks Review*, September, 1964, pp. 3–25.

Mundell, Robert A. "The International Disequilibrium System." *Kyklos* 14 (1961): 154–172.

Mundell, Robert A. "The Appropriate Use of Monetary and Fiscal Policy Under Fixed Exchange Rates." *IMF Staff Papers* 9 (March, 1962): 70–77.

Mundell, Robert A. "Capital Mobility and Stabilization Policy Under Fixed and Flexible Exchange Rates." *Canadian Journal of Economics and Political Science* 29 (November, 1963): 475–485.

Rueff, Jacques. "The West is Risking a Credit Collapse." *Fortune*, July, 1961, pp. 126–127, 262–268.

Rushing, Philip. "The Reciprocal Currency Arrangements." *New England Economic Review*, November/December, 1972, pp. 3–15.

Sellekaerts, W., and Sellekaerts, B. "Balance of Payments Deficits, the Adjustment Cost, and the Optimum Level of International Reserves." *Weltwirtschaftliches Archiv*, vol. 109, pt. 1 (1973), pp. 1–17.

Simon, M. "The Hot-Money Movement and the Private Exchange Pool Proposal of 1896." *Journal of Economic History* 20 (March, 1960): 31–50.

"Swaps: Tool to Promote Orderly Exchange Markets Again in Use." *IMF Survey*, December 17, 1973, pp. 365–366.

Triffin, Robert. "The Coexistence of Three Types of Reserve Assets." *Banca Nazionale del lavoro Quarterly Review*, June, 1967, pp. 107–134.

Walker, C. H. "The Working of the Pre-War Gold Standard." *Review of Economic Studies* 1–2 (1933–1935): 196–209.

Williamson, John. "International Liquidity: A Survey." *Economic*

Journal 83 (September, 1973): 685–746.

Williamson, John. "Need for Solution to Valuation of SDRs Has Grown with Wider Use of Floating." *IMF Survey,* February 4, 1974, pp. 40–41.

Wittich, Günter, and Shiratori, Masaki. "The Snake in the Tunnel." *Finance and Development,* June, 1973, pp. 9–13, 38.   ..

Yeager, Leland B. "The Triffin Plan: Diagnosis, Remedy, and Alternatives." *Kyklos* 14 (1961): 285–312.

Yeager, Leland B. "A Skeptical View of the 'Band' Proposal." *National Banking Review* 4 (March, 1967): 291–297.

MONOGRAPHS

Bloomfield, Arthur I. *Short-Term Capital Movements Under the Pre-1914 Gold Standard.* Studies in International Finance, no. 11. Princeton: International Finance Section, 1963.

Cohen, Benjamin J. *Adjustment Costs and the Distribution of New Reserves.* Studies in International Finance, no. 18. Princeton: International Finance Section, 1966.

Flanders, M. J. *The Demand for International Reserves.* Studies in International Finance, no. 27. Princeton: International Finance Section, 1971.

Flemming, J. M. *Towards Assessing the Need for International Reserves.* Essays in International Finance, no. 58. Princeton: International Finance Section, 1967.

Haberler, Gottfried. *Prospects for the Dollar Standard.* Reprint

no. 3. Washington: American Enterprise Institute, 1972.

Halm, George N. *The Band Proposals: The Limits of Permissible Exchange Rate Variations.* Special Papers in International Finance, no. 6. Princeton: International Finance Section, 1965.

Krause, Lawrence B. *Fixed, Flexible, and Gliding Exchange Rates,* no. 205. Washington: American Enterprise Institute, 1971.

Lindert, Peter H. *Key Currencies and Gold: 1900–1913.* Studies in International Finance, no. 24. Princeton: International Finance Section, 1969.

Lutz, Friedrich A. *The Keynes and White Papers.* Essays in International Finance, no. 1. Princeton: International Section, 1943.

Machlup, Fritz. *Plans for Reform of the International Monetary System.* Special Papers in International Finance, no. 3. Princeton: International Finance Section, 1962.

Machlup, Fritz. *The Need for Monetary Reserves.* Reprints in International Finance, no. 5. Princeton: International Finance Section, 1966.

McKinnon, Ronald I. *Private and Official International Money: The Case for the Dollar.* Essays in International Finance, no. 74. Princeton: International Finance Section, 1969.

Plumptre, A. F. *Exchange-Rate Policy: Experience With Canada's Floating Rate.* Essays in International Finance, no. 81. Princeton: International Finance Section, 1970.

Salant, Walter S. *Practical Techniques for Assessing the Need for Reserves.* Reprint no. 198.

Washington: The Brookings Institution, 1971.

Scitovsky, Tibor. *Requirements of an International Reserve System.* Essays in International Finance, no. 49. Princeton: International Finance Section, 1965.

Williamson, John. *The Crawling Peg.* Essays in International Finance, no. 50. Princeton: International Finance Section, 1965.

Williamson, John. *The Choice of a Pivot for Parities.* Essays in International Finance, no. 90. Princeton: International Finance Section, 1971.

GOVERNMENT PUBLICATIONS

Annual Report. Washington: International Monetary Fund, 1963.

Culbertson, J. M. "Alternative International Monetary Systems." *Recent Changes in Monetary Policy and Balance of Payments Problems.* Hearings Before the Committee on Banking and Currency, 88th Congress, First Session. Washington: Government Printing Offices, 1963, pp. 331–344.

International Financial Statistics. Washington: International Monetary Fund, September, 1973.

Index